V
L
O
E
D

Memory landscapes between Essex and the Netherlands

LUCIA DOVE

VLOED
Lucia Dove

Published by Dunlin Press in 2021

Dunlin Press
Wivenhoe, Essex
dunlinpress.com | @dunlinpress

A CIP record of this book is available from the British Library.

ISBN: 978-0-9931259-8-0

Set in FreightText Pro and Vanitas.
Unless otherwise stated all photography by Lucia Dove.
Cover, illustrations and design by Ella Johnston.

Of late here hath bene such a tide heire as hath overflowen al medowes and marshses. All th'Isle of Dogges, al Plumsted marshe, al Sheppey, Foulnes in Essex, and al the sea cost was quite drowned. We here that it hath done no lesse harm in Flandres, Holland, and Zellaund, but much more. For townes and cities have ben their drouned.

SITES AND SPECIFICS

INITIAL OBSERVATIONS

Encounters are servants to memory, to history and to commemoration, and they lead us to a point at which a forgotten disaster can be perceived anew, or a catastrophe that has ebbed away can come back upon us like a tidal wave.

THOMAS ELSAESSER, 2013

A desire to write about my home of Southend-on-Sea, having predominately lived in the areas of Westcliff, Chalkwell and Leigh, has grown with the knowledge that to do so effectively requires a type of understanding of the place itself, rather than of my place in it. In September 2018, a year and six months after I had moved to Amsterdam, I made the following observation:

'The Essex solitary', a condition that thrives on incongruity, as defined by Tim Burrows in his opening essay to the publication *Radical Essex*, is the reason I'm yet to write a poem (that works) on Southend and its surrounding landscapes – language feels stifled and 'outside of things' whenever I try.

What I have come to realise, is that the language I was using to translate my often overwhelming feelings about home at the expansive, leaking, historic mouth of the Thames was too obvious. Maybe it still is. But my move to the Netherlands stirred in me something that was not obvious at all: through attempting to settle somewhat in a new country, I have become better equipped, practically and emotionally, to comprehend my position between the two places. I believe this is to do with their aligned landscapes. Geographically close to one another, Essex, Suffolk and Norfolk share the shallow North Sea basin with the west of the Netherlands – indeed the two were once connected by the ancient sunken land mass known as Doggerland. From the end of the last ice age, through the Roman period to the present day, a long shared history connects the two places. The North Sea Flood of 1953 is one such event that has deeply affected national and local consciousnesses in both countries. In the Netherlands, the devastation was felt (and is still felt) all across the country. In the UK, the flood's legacy lies not at the national level but locally in places such as Canvey Island, where it remains an integral element of its memory landscape. There is so much to say about the two countries: their shared colonial histories; of colonisation and migration on a wider scale; and of bordered (wet)lands. There are issues with how water is dealt with, how it is drained and displaced to striate and monetise land. Those who perished from the Great Flood in 1953, particularly in those areas in the UK most affected (Jaywick, Harwich and Canvey Island), were from a disadvantaged economic position, living in poorly made houses after an unfair allocation of resources following World War II. As the aphorism goes, the rich live on the hill, the poor by the (ever rising) water.

As such, the way I have tried to write about the flood is not solely to recount the chronological orderings of the event. Rather, it is to respond to a relationship between people and place, with the support of the writers and artists who have influenced my understanding of memory landscapes, the lived environment and fluidity. With this acquired knowledge and new *woordenschat* – the Dutch term for vocabulary that translates directly as 'word treasure' – I hope to offer my response to the historical, natural, social and cultural encounters of the *watersnoodramp*, the Great Flood of 1953.

January 2021

Truth is the criterion of historical study; but its impelling motive is poetic. Its poetry consists in its being true.[1]

G.M. TREVELYAN, 1942

SOUTHEND-ON-SEA

The estuary is filling up like a bathtub. Water discharges and displaces into the surrounding land.

How is the Thames estuary perceived by those who live and work along its foreshores, sandbanks and sea walls? When the sky is bright and you look out towards the Isle of Grain or Sheppey, or to the all familiar enveloping grey, do you feel as if you are standing on a line or on an edge?

I have been trying to unthink the Essex coastline in the interest of erasure. To undefine a landscape so familiar to oneself is not an easy thing to do, but to be able to consider the Essex estuaries – with their multitude of islands, creeks and rivers that braid and leak into each other, and with all the life that has flourished and been taken by it – it becomes a necessary task. The materiality of water and its effect on land is what makes it a radical substance; its constant movement demands a dynamic reaction of us. Lindsay Bremner's practice of *unthinking*

---

1 G.M. Trevelyan in 1942, in Hilda Grieve, *The Great Tide* (Essex County Council, 1959).

coastlines allows us to see beyond demarcated land and into a flowing zone. This is necessary for understanding how people live and move through these zones.[2]

Like Bremner, let us think about fluidity, think fluidly on the material substances, on the actual things that flow:

armies, armadas, bodies (alive, dead), women, men, children, convicts, windsurfers, kitesurfers, swimmers, day-trippers, tourists, fishermen, prisoners, the sick, the healthy, the lost, the found, the saved, the murdered;

container ships, cargo, Dutch barges, Thames barges, trawlers, prefabs, pleasure boats, caravans, war ships;

whales, fish, crab, mussels, jellyfish, worms, seaweed, algae;

birds, wild fowl, sea mews, roysten crows, wild ducks, herons, swans, curlew, dunlin, brent geese, goods;

waste, tampons, sanitary towels, cocaine, plastics, ceramics, bombs (unexploded, exploded);

---

2 In the research project *Monsoon Assemblages* that works to 'reframe understandings of climate change in monsoon cities in South Asia', project leader Lindsay Bremner proposes that the monsoon, rather than being 'a natural meteorological system outside of and distinct from society [...] is a co-production of physical and social dynamics entangled within historic lived environments that can be analysed, worked with, shaped and changed.' Lindsay Bremner 'On Monsoon Assemblages' in *Migrant 3: Flowing Grounds* (Migrant Journal, 2017) p91.

weather, wind, water, sand, mud, sun, rain, fog, storm;

floods, fluids

that 'flow', 'spill', 'run out', 'splash', 'pour over', 'leak', 'flood', 'spray', 'drip', 'seep', 'ooze'; unlike solids, they are not easily stopped – they pass around some obstacles, dissolve some others and bore or soak their way through others still. From the meeting with solids they emerge unscathed, while the solids they have met, if they stay solid, are changed – get moist or drenched.[3]

Our intimacies with water are always decided by the water and landscape with which we associate ourselves. Sometimes we might believe that we have shaped the water but it is the water that has given us shape. If we see water as a radical material substance, we realise that it represents both the substantive – our social, political, cultural heritages – and the representational – the fluidity of our dreams, memories, perceptions and meanings.

The concept of a memory landscape incorporates collective knowledge associated with the idea of landscape from a cultural, socioeconomic and historical perspective. It gives clarity to the understanding of a coastal landscape that is defined by water. Norbert Fischer writes how regionally specific experiences of maritime death and grief are materialised and perceived. Memories are sedimented into the landscape. This process depends on our experiences and changing reactions in how

3 Zygmunt Bauman, *Liquid Modernity* (Polity Press, 2000) p2.

we deal with the threatening sea, which are built upon by our different social needs.

Fischer writes: 'Under these conditions, the coastal landscape has been repeatedly reconfigured through the interaction of culture, mentality and society.'[4]

It is in this interaction, the interconnectivity of our existence under the perpetually changing conditions and structure of the sea, that our landscape, and the landscape of this book, takes place. The study of landscape is ambiguous and flowable. Like the zones that people from different landscapes inhabit and move through, in order to study landscape it must be recognised that there is no fixed definition. It is this unbounded approach of accessing two particular landscapes, and the relationship between them, that I am interested in.

On the Saturday night of the 31st of January and the Sunday morning of the 1st of February 1953, a great flood devastated Scotland, England, Belgium and the Netherlands. It killed more than 2,550 people.

---

4 Norbert Fischer, 'Maritime Death, Memory and Landscape' in *Waddenland Outstanding* (Amsterdam University Press, 2018) p171.

Scotland   19

Belgium   28

England   307

North Sea   361

The Netherlands   1,836

(The animals and the unidentified and the unaccounted for)

My understanding of this history could not have been told without Hilda Grieve (b. 1913, d. 1993) who was senior assistant archivist at the Essex Record Office at the time she wrote her monumental historical account of the flood, *The Great Tide*, in 1959. Commissioned by Essex County Council and considered as one of the most important pieces of social commentary of our time, the book maps out in immense detail the events leading up to the flood and its aftermath. In it, Grieve historically foregrounds the area's vulnerability to flooding – how these lands and its inhabitants have long suffered a watery history soaked through and through and through.

Despite growing up in Southend, I had never heard of the 1953 flood. We had local history school trips whilst attending primary and secondary school: to the fishing village Old Leigh to learn about the local witch Sarah Moore, to Hadleigh Castle, and even to London's Tate Britain to see John Constable's *Sketch for Hadleigh Castle*. But to the best of my memory and to my regret, the flood never received any attention. It might have been different if I had been raised on Canvey Island where 13,000 people were evacuated and 58 people died – the highest number of lives taken by the flood in the UK.

Burial party

As a young woman she worked in the local museum.
Since Kings have been unearthed. Knees drawn up
to where the bellybutton should be. Loss of perspective.
Once the jetty has sunk beneath what will you hold
your pencil to? Boudica drawn in the sand.
Lunch in vans. Warm fistfuls of the wrong change.
Still car sick. A makeshift fairground in her own kitchen.
A teenager punching the water arcade. Ding ding ding.
Strapped to an electric chair, she catches a fish on her lap.
Amidst fear, you're out of pocket, or you are at the end
of a long crane, or you are held by a wet claw. We discover
another King and tarmac over it. Calculating the inventory
of what we had hoped we would be buried with: a knife,
a pencil, the tide times and a pair of clean, dry knickers.

HOLLAND

HOLLAND

Beyond the black grounds the areas of sand and silt are to be found running in broad strips parallel with the shore line of the islands. Between the areas of sand and silt may be found the low ridges of sand and shell. These alternating areas of bands of sand and silt, and sand and shell occur until the channel known as the West Swin is reached.

The term 'swin' means to the islanders a large channel in which there is water at any state of the tide.[5]

I am flying over a flat veil of cloud between the Netherlands and England. I am looking over Doggerland at dusk. A wet and undulating land with dark pockets that you would fall right through if you stepped short. All blue and all green. I know that the lights of boats shining beneath are from another world altogether. A future one, where the swell of the North Sea would go onto shape, and keep re-shaping, so much of what is important to me now. The land is built of black sand and shell

---

5 P.A. and D.P. Arnold on behalf of the Foulness Island Residents Committee, *FOULNESS* (1969) p4. The word 'swin' derives from the Old English meaning a creek or a channel. It was published as 'Swyn' in 1365, the same word 'zwin' occurs in Dutch.

and sand and silt and shell and silt and probably poor dogs scouring low areas for silt. If I were to fall through its sandy holes I would land with a splash into the North Sea rising. Faster than anyone could have ever imagined. And would my motion be enough to alter the current state of its watery disposition? And if not mine, then some other's perhaps, or some other thing? All blue and all green.

I am in so many layers of black cloud.

I am so sure that we are flying over Southend. I almost wave. But it seems so small and dream-like. The layout is all there. The pier visible. The lights extending right out into the water in the way that they do, water lapping around its supports. But it is so small. Is it really Southend? We have flown past it now. It must be another seaside town, with another pier, really much smaller, probably a lot more vulnerable to flooding.

But perhaps not.

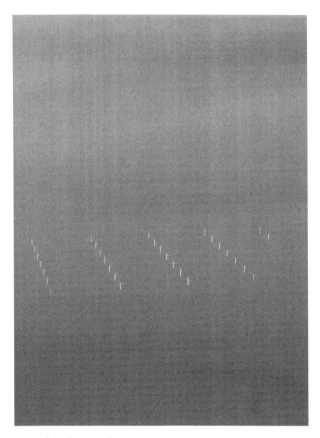

Somewhere between homes, 2019

The flight between Southend and the Netherlands often feels like a dream, nebulous and gauze-like.[6] I take the EasyJet 21:55 from Schiphol to London Southend on a Thursday evening and return on Sunday evening 19:20. In the summer the sky feels as if it is softly sinking beneath me with the falling light. In the winter everything has already sunk and I am able to see very little. One such evening, the German writer W.G. Sebald sat on Gunhill in Southwold, Suffolk, looking out to the North Sea. It is submerged memories, he writes, that give to dreams their curious air of hyper-reality. The something else, 'through which everything one sees in a dream seems, paradoxically, much clearer'. Despite putting my feelings on this strange phenomenon into words, it is beyond even Sebald's understanding. So too, he writes, is believing that one year earlier he was looking across to England, sat on a beach in Scheveningen, Holland.

The development of (London) Southend Airport as an international airport was completed in time for the 2012 Olympics that were held in Stratford in East London. Connected by the newly improved Greater Anglia railway line, passengers flying into Southend could be at the Olympic stadium within 45 minutes. The airport was a crucial component of London's Olympic bid and Southend was to play an even bigger part in becoming an official Olympic venue. Hadleigh Farm, overlooking the Thames Estuary, owned by the Salvation Army and home to the ruins of the high medieval Hadleigh Castle, was the best stadium nature could offer for mountain biking with a good connection from London.

---

6 W.G. Sebald, *The Rings of Saturn* (New Directions, 1979) p80.

International flights are in operation out of the small Rochford airport. People from Southend, on the whole, are proud of this airport. Three years after moving to the Netherlands, when I am still explaining my motivations for moving here, I find myself always mentioning how easy it is for me to 'fly back home' with Schiphol airport 45 kilometres away and my parents' house a 10-minute drive from the airport, responses always come with enthusiastic nods of approval for how handy the airport is.

Once, when I arrived at border control in Southend and handed over my passport, the border guard looked at it, then at me, back at the passport, back at me and said, 'Wow, you really are local.'

He said this because what remains of the hospital where I was born sits at the end of the runway. The Grade II listed white chimney of the old boiler house at Rochford Hospital stands as a stoic reminder of the place where so many were born. It was the only maternity unit in the local area before being transferred to Southend in 1995. It was subsequently demolished, a year after I was born there. Flying home then, to either one of my homes, means travelling to and from the almost exact location where I came into the world.

Rochford Hospital, 2020

I moved to Amsterdam in March 2017. For a long, continuous time I felt homesick in a very unspecific way. I didn't miss a certain food or particular smell; I couldn't satiate my feeling of loss through calls with family or listening to British radio. Though it's true that moving to another country where you do not know anyone or speak the language is an isolating experience, for me, more than anything I felt physically out of place. This feeling was somewhat mollified once I'd travelled out of the city of Amsterdam and visited places like the Soesterduinen in the province of Utrecht, an expanse of man-made sand dunes and forest, or travelling by train through the flat lands to the north.

It was once I had travelled to Friesland, a province in the north of the Netherlands, when I felt the homesickness abate. The landscape was so like that of the place I considered home.

In Zwarte Haan, one of the villages looking toward to the Wadden Islands of Terschelling and Ameland, a sign board at the bottom of a manmade dune leading to the water described the place, 'black swan', as 'the start of the world'. It echoed a description of Southend that I'd seen before. In his essay 'Essex, An Island off London', Tim Burrows, who also grew up in Southend, writes how during his youth 'Southend seemed at the edge of nowhere, the end of the line, but here', he adds, 'it could have been a twinkling beginning.'[7]

This not knowing if a landscape signals the start or the end, the deliberate unthinking of a coastline, the thinking that water and

---

7 Tim Burrows, 'Essex, An Island off London' in *Somesuch Stories 3*, (Somesuch, 2017) p117.

landscape approximates 'Nothing'[8], are all valuable perspectives when engaging with landscape. Perspectives on landscape are inherently ambiguous and pop up anywhere, often in an unpredictable manner.[9] Travelling out of the province of North Holland and into that of Utrecht, Friesland and finally to Zeeland, I feel a more welcome, though not necessarily pleasant, isolation. It is an isolation that I recognise while exploring Essex, because with Essex, as with any place you grow up in, there is always more to explore. Tim Burrows writes of 'the Essex solitary' in his chapter 'The Essex Escape' in the publication *Radical Essex*, a term he uses to describe the particular feeling of being decidedly outside of things. It is, he writes, 'a condition that thrives on incongruity; despite the county's closeness to the city, it is still possible to feel the eeriness a sudden emptying of urban markers brings.'[10] These experiences came as small revelations to me and contributed to my slow settling in the Netherlands (though it is one that is still sinking, three years on). When I first moved, I watched a documentary about Dutch history in Dutch with English subtitles, on my laptop in bed, mice scratching away in the Amsterdam apartment's old walls.

---

8 'For what is water, children, which seeks to make all things level, which has no taste or colour of its own, but a liquid form of Nothing? And what are the Fens, which so imitate in their levelness the natural dispositions of water, but a landscape which, of all landscapes, most approximates Nothing?'. Graham Swift, *Waterland* (Picador, 2015) p20. I am increasingly interested in the idea of Nothing. In the first line of a collaborative poem by Sophie Collins and Daisy Lafarge (2019), it is written: 'The only way to be accurate, I think, is to say nothing.'
9 Christopher Tilley and Kate Cameron-Daum, 'The anthropology of landscape: materiality, embodiment, contestation and emotion' in *An Anthropology of Landscape*, (UCL Press, 2017) p1.
10 Tim Burrows, 'The Essex Escape: A Partial History' in *Radical Essex*, (Focal Point Gallery, 2018) p9.

'Abnormal,' the flood was described. Nearly 2,000 people.

Black and white images of people grouped together, supporting one another as the supports of their houses were torn away. Dead animals, children. And in the same cold hours, the same water breaking in and spreading down the southeast coastline towards Essex.

FOULNESS ISLAND

FOULNESS ISLAND

silt

    mud
    peat

       silt

    mud
       peat

   silt

modder
      peat   slib
            modder
               veen
silt
   modder
      peat

     slib
    mud   veen

Alternating layers of silt (mud deposited by water) and peat (vegetation decomposed by water) in Essex, laid bare when excavation has been carried out during the construction of coastal works such as docks, gas works and power stations. These mark alternating periods of advance and retreat by the sea.

35

Soil Strata for Great Burwood

The topsoil is a natural
Build up mainly early
C20th finds were recovered
From this level.

Level I

The soil at this level appears to have
Been brought to the site to
Level the area prior to the
C17th building construction.
It would seem most likely
From the make up of this
Strata level that the soil comes
at the time when the local
Pond was being constructed.
The finds at this level are
Mainly from the late C17th
However we do find in certain
Areas of the site earlier and later
Finds, this we believe is due to
Disturbance from modern C20th
Rubbish pits which were dug
After the original Gt. Burwood
Was demolished.

Level II

This is what is known as natural,
For this area that means a sandy
Type of soil lightish brown in colour
The C14th occupation is found at this level.

Information sheet on display at Foulness Island Heritage Centre, which is only open to the public for seven days of the year.

Two thousand years of history can be told through Essex tidal mud. The beginning of Hilda Grieve's *The Great Tide* is dedicated to how the sea has steadily encroached upon the land since Roman times. Excavations made during the building of docks in the River Thames since the Industrial Revolution have uncovered Roman artefacts. In many sites throughout Essex, salt marshes preserved under peat layers are home to occupational remains of the Stone and Bronze ages. Fire-hearths over 1,900 years old were uncovered on Canvey Island. The stumps of salt-intolerant yew trees were found buried in silt. According to Grieve, they must have grown when the land stood at least 15ft higher than it is now.[11]

It is not just the stumps of trees buried below salt marsh and mud. In 1327, an Essex hamlet called Milton was lost to the rising sea. A small settlement on the foreshore, without a church, without God. Land and tenants flooded. The town of Dunwich, one of the most important ports in Europe during the Middle Ages, also disappeared, the last of it 1919.

Salt preserves the ribs of shipwrecks. Stubborn alluvial material reveals ancient markers now slightly out of plumb. It is both man and tides that make islands. The geological make-up of these lands, where we walk, plunge out of boats moored up the mud bank, where we play, work, buy-up these lands, these lands seep through us until man is breached and reclaimed. 'Silt: which shapes and undermines continents; which demolishes as it builds; which is simultaneous accretion and erosion; neither progress nor decay.'[12]

---

11 Hilda Grieve, *The Great Tide* (Essex County Council, 1959) p2-3.
12 Graham Swift, *Waterland* (Picador, 2015) p16.

All Saints Church (1906). ©Dunwich Museum 2020

it, too, slipped over the cliff edge

St James, St Leonard, St Martin, St Batholomew, St Michael,
St Patrick, St Mary, St John, St Peter, St Nicholas, St Felix

churches, monasteries, convents, hospitals

shipyards, fortifications, fisheries, merchant fleets

earth, loam, stone, alluvial sand, gravel

dozens of windmills, walls, wells

1285, 1328, 1919

chimney shafts, stacks, towers

churchyards, many thousand souls, bones of the dead, dead flowers

Alternating layers and material goods of Dunwich over time.

Forty square miles of the lower Thames marshes are the natural flood-plain of the Thames. The word flood-plain must be interpreted literally, for while the embanking restricts the lateral development of a tide it increases the heights of the tide, including of course the highest tide. These will inevitably spill over into parts of the flood-plain.[13]

In the late 16th century Foulness had changed from a projecting headland into an island through a great tide. It is now the largest of the Essex islands.

On Foulness, at the end of one end of the ancient Broomway path, just beyond the sea wall, you will find the grassy foundations of a bungalow, visible not from its bricks and concrete, but from the high weeds and flowers tangling over what would have been the windows and roof of Mrs Rawlings' home, growing from her garden. The shrubs reminded me of photographs I'd seen from 1953 taken in Zeeland: a fine but rusting gate leading to an empty field where a house once stood. A remnant of the flood, a monument. Mrs Rawlings was one of the two women to have died on Foulness from the great flood of 1953. Both were widows and both were called Mrs Rawlings: Bertha Rawlings and Violet Rawlings.

---

13 In 1969, P.A. and D.P. Arnold, on behalf of the Foulness Island Residents Committee, prepared a pamphlet entitled *FOULNESS* in order to present 'a fair summary of the true facts concerning the geology, geography, history and industry of the area.' It was created in response to misleading statements about the area surrounding the suggestion of Foulness or the Maplin Sands as a possible site for London's third airport. In the pamphlet, the authors write of rising sea levels, the composition of the land, and quote a paper in the *Journal of the Institute of Navigation* that states that 'the whole of the sands in the Thames Estuary may be considered unconsolidated and that they are continually moving.'

Swept

The mystery was not that it had been snowing but that the snow was of the same composition and of the same temperature as the water.

Looking outside your window to see sweeping water is not the same as seeing a fresh covering of snow.

All farmhouses are lonely

In the basement they found
a family, waiting for the end

in a farmhouse in Drenthe.
Just as on Foulness, waiting
for news of someone's death.

Letter

1/
Altho' I was out sorting clothes
on a bench in our garden
for the most of it, so my
memory tells me, sister
and brother helped mother
on a Sunday morning. I,
just-turned teenager,
pairing socks and figuring
handmedowns to strangers,
our neighbours, mum would
have us say. Neighbour's needs.
Neighbours wearing only what
they wore when rescued.
The Is. was below sea level

2/
Come Mon., I'm at school you see,
the severity of the floods
was brought home to me.
We did not know what we had

3/
Shoeburyness to Foulness Is.,
Burnham-on-Crouch
thence to London. Dot and I,
both eighty now, are still friends.
Our tales are enormous. Well,
her house on Foulness flooded.
Come Mon., after more than a week,
she returned. I can't remember
the exact emotion.
On seeing her alive, school mistress asks,
'Why are you not wearing your uniform?'
She had lost EVERYTHING

4/
1963, bought a
house in Gt.
Wakering.
Living room
floodline
marked 3-4ft

5/
There comes a time
when we move to the far-end
of somewhere. We either edge
away or closer to low lying land.
Distance measured in approximation
of how far you are from a sea wall.
People here measure their time by
before or after the flood.
Those living in the Nissen huts died,
so I've been told by Thames Barger
'The Boy'

6/
Altho' I was only a teen
I remember thinking how
this will be remembered.
Cold, wet and frightened!

7/
I was writing to a Dutch girl
who lived in Amsterdam. Penfriends.
She had relatives in the flooded areas
who were displaced. I met some of them,
tho' I believe many had lost their lives.

She took me to the flooded place five
years later. My friend died last year,
I no longer receive any news

8/
My husband's father Tom,
Police Constable, was not known
to have survived or died.
Come Mon., young T was called
out of class and told
to go home, old T
had been found safe and well.
A wonderful outcome!

Based on a letter to Miss Lucia Dove from Mrs Doreen Baker and Mr Tony
Baker. The letter was accompanied with a photocopy of a Commendation
for the MOD Police Constable Tom Baker, dated 19th February, 1953.
It reads:

*Commended by the Chief Constable, War Department Constabulary, for
outstanding devotion to duty in the A.R.E., Area, on the night 31st January/1st
February 1953, in that he although realising the extreme gravity of the Flood
Situation remained at his post, regardless of his own safety, without light – heat
– or food until rescued at about 9.20.am on 2nd February. This Officer returned
to Shoeburyness bringing all keys with him after securing his various charges.*

*Signed by Chief Constable and sent from the Chief Constable's Office, War
Department Constabulary, Room 515 Northumberland House, The War Office,
London, S.W.1.*

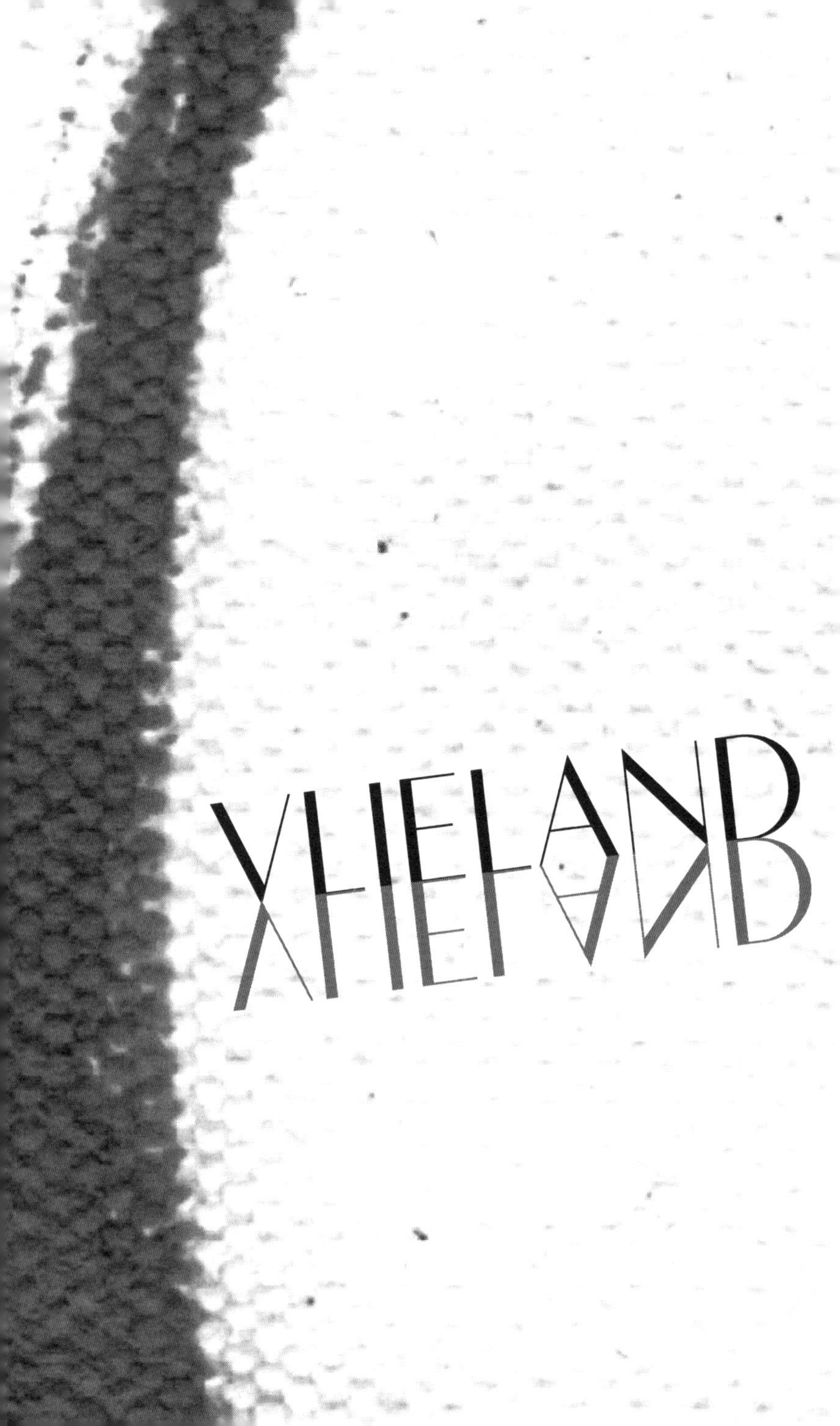

VLIELAND

After Joure, Vlieland was one of first places I visited in Friesland. I distinctly remember the childlike excitement at arriving at the passenger ferry terminal in Harlingen and waiting to board the boat. It had been a long time since I'd been on a boat, which I remember struck me as odd considering I had lived by the sea my whole life. If I'd been on a boat anywhere, it wasn't in Southend. Funny then, that the harbour on Vlieland should remind me so much of my home, with the bobbing sailboats and the bustle of a seafront. I had journeyed to the island alone on a late Thursday evening on the last day of August 2017, feeling particularly lucky. I was met by a friend and two bicycles. I am sure my mind in hindsight has softened the edges of how I really felt that weekend – homseick, most likely – but for me it was blissful to discover this new place that I have returned to each year since. The island, the smallest of all the West Frisian Islands, is only accessible on foot (or bike) as cars are only allowed for residents. The only village on the island is Oost-Vlieland (East Vlieland). With a population of around 1,100, Vlieland is the second least densely populated municipality in the country. Like all places in the Netherlands, the history of Vlieland is formed by water – it is formed by the sea and formed by floods.[14] Oost-Vlieland was once not the only village on Vlieland. West-Vlieland, slowly encroached upon by the sea and falling sand dunes, was the main trading village on the island. By the late 1600s the village was on the beach. Farmers allowed their cattle to graze on the dunes, weakening them until the dunes could no longer hold against large storms. In 1714 the church was swallowed by waves and in 1729 the village was abandoned; its sandy remains lie under where the Vliehors is today. The Vliehors is a 25-kilometre extended area of beach – the largest sand plain in Northwestern Europe that is still inundated by high water levels due to low-lying sandbanks. While part of the Vliehors is a nature reserve, one area has long been used for military training by the Royal Netherlands Air Force and NATO, who practice with ammunition and explosive charges. This sandy outreach was once populated with farmers, fishermen, traders and families, but now the military forbids public access to the site during the week. Across the North Sea in Essex, a similar though much stricter situation exists on Foulness Island, an area of just under 25 kilometres which is owned by the Ministry of Defence and protected by security and defence contractors QinetiQ. Access onto the island is only possible for employees and the handful of residents who live there. But every first Sunday of the month, from April

---

14 Although there were some victims of the 1953 flood on the Wadden Sea island of Texel, the intrinsic relationship between the Wadden Sea region and flooding extends throughout history. Floods have not only formed the geographical elements of the landscape but also its cultural consciousness. Describing those who have died as a result of flooding as 'victims' is emotionally and intellectually significant as it bolsters the rhetoric of floods as an invasion – of our battle against the sea, of survival and of loss. It is this concept that has allowed (and continues to allow) engineers to profit from 'taming' 'wild' marshland and tidal landscapes.

to October, people can visit the Foulness Island Heritage Centre. The volunteers there arrange flora and fauna tractor and trailer rides around the island; comparable perhaps with Vliehors's 'Vliehors Express', but the latter without a security car following you around, as I experienced on the tractor ride I took last summer. The Vliehors Express takes visitors to the Rescue House situated in the middle of the Vliehors, formerly a refuge for the stranded and now a beachcombing museum. A place for the lost and found.

As one of the Frisian Islands, Vlieland is on the border of two seas, the North and the Wadden Sea. The eastern saltmarsh – home to the ferry terminal, the first place I tried poffertjes (small pillows of fried dough served with butter and powder sugar) and Vlieland's lighthouse – looks to the Wadden Sea. The sea itself is a conservation area, a tidal zone of water and saltmarsh which holds a place on the World Heritage List as a natural area of Outstanding Universal Value. The island is bordered to the north by the North Sea. The West Frisian Islands were once a combined sandbank but have separated over time, though they still provide an important barrier to protect the mainland coast. That this sandbank broke up into multiple islands[15] and still protects the mainland coast is a striking example of how the process of *undoing* in landscape does not necessarily mean that it loses purpose or cultural importance. The Wadden Sea region is considered unique in that it is 'the geographical outcome of the struggle of an "amphibious" society (having both an agrarian and maritime character) with and within a rich and

---

15 There are around 50 islands in the whole Wadden Sea region, stretching across the coasts of the Netherlands, Germany and Denmark, the majority of which form a barrier separating the Wadden from the North Sea.

fertile, though hazardous, maritime environment.'[16] The entire area has been formed in its interaction between nature and human and though the islands themselves are separated by the beautiful creations of a tidal environment, estuaries and creeks, the area is considered to 'nevertheless form one contiguous, coherent landscape with a history that can be traced back some 3,000 years.'[17]

Vlieland

Het meisje in de
donker blauwe rok,
verbrande rode bloes,
gele hoofddoek in haar haar
met een dikke abrikoos

Southend

The girl in the
dark blue skirt,
burnt red blouse,
yellow headscarf in her hair
with a fat apricot

---

16 'Comparative Analysis of the Landscape and Cultural Heritage of the Wadden Sea Region' (Essex County Council, 2010) p12.
17 Ibid.

Barges protecting the saltmarsh at Bradwell Shell Bank Nature Reserve, Essex

The Wadden Islands, © OpenStreetMap Authors, CC-BY-SA

Through *eb en vloed* (ebb and flow), farmers in the early Middle Ages would use the salt marsh and peat area between Vlieland and Friesland for pasture, and it was still possible to cross this area of the tidal Wadden Sea up until the 19th century. Though it is no surprise to me because of the similarities between this landscape and that of the Thames estuary, I was still interested to learn that in 2010 Essex County Council published a Comparative Analysis of the Landscape and Cultural Heritage of the Wadden Sea Region with the aim to determine how unique the cultural landscape of the Wadden Sea Region is internationally.[18] Crucially, the study is concerned with how the natural elements of the region have formed its cultural identity. The formation of the landscape, though it may have originally taken shape through natural processes such as storm surges and floods,[19] has since been 'humanity that adapted and shaped, destroyed and rebuilt, by deliberate planning as well as through trial and error, these maritime lands creating the landscape we see today.'[20] In outlining their comparative approach to the study, the authors assembled a list of areas, mainly wetland

---

18 'Wad' itself means shallow or fordable place, presumably derived from the possibility, in many places, to cross this sea on foot at ebb-tides.' 'Comparative Analysis of the Landscape and Cultural Heritage of the Wadden Sea Region' (Essex County Council, 2010) p26.
19 On the 13–14th of December 1287, Vlieland was permanently separated from the Frisian mainland by the St. Lucia's flood. This flood, one of the most catastrophic in the history of the Netherlands, can perhaps be considered on the same disastrous level as the one in 1953 in terms of lasting effects. According to the chronicles of an Abbey in Witterwierum, the St. Lucia flood caused the deaths of 50,000 people and although these figures are probably exaggerated, given the small population size at that time, the flood formed the Wadden Sea (Waternoodsmuseum board).
20 'Comparative Analysis of the Landscape and Cultural Heritage of the Wadden Sea Region' (Essex County Council, 2010) p26.

landscapes, which also have a distinct cultural aspect to them. In finding these comparative sites they found that though qualities of the cultural landscape of the Wadden Sea region existed in other places, nowhere had all of the qualities, confirming both the uniqueness of the region but, crucially, that the differences between the sites prove to be as important as the similarities.[21] Along with 14 other areas, the Greater Thames Estuary was listed as a site of comparative interest to the Wadden Sea region. The site was scored under seven criteria that were drawn out from the analysis of the cultural significance of the Wadden Sea. The points of comparison were: time-depth; integrity of cultural landscape; level of archaeological and documentary evidence; degree of adaptation of the natural landscape; associative cultural significance; extent of cultural landscape; and authenticity. After the Wadden Sea region (which scored 28), the Greater Thames Estuary ranks fourth in the table with a score of 22. It sits between the other two UK sites of Romney Marsh (Kent and East Sussex) and The Wash (Norfolk and Lincolnshire). The Greater Thames Estuary shares the same score as the Wadden Sea region in Level of archaeological and documentary evidence available and Associative cultural significance[22], the report summaries the area: 'Although the

---

21 'Comparative Analysis of the Landscape and Cultural Heritage of the Wadden Sea Region' (Essex County Council, 2010) p14–15.
22 Associative cultural significance refers partly to the technological aspect of land reclamation but also the link with the cultural concept of a struggle against the sea and the taming of nature. Interestingly, the report goes on to describe a further attribute of associative cultural significance: that of the development of aesthetics in the Enlightenment and the aesthetics of the sublime as testified by artists and writers during the first half of the 20th century, whose work paved the way, along with the development of railways, for tourism in the Wadden Sea region (and the Greater Thames Estuary).

Greater Thames Estuary, The Wash and Romney Marsh are all notable coastal marsh areas, with long and complex histories, a significant portion of their landscape history and development is dependent on the introduction of land reclamation knowledge and technologies that originated in the Wadden Sea area, and adjacent parts of the Netherlands.'[23]

From this I can conclude that without Friesland and the Wadden Sea region, the home of Vlieland, where I felt at home upon my first visit, that my home of Southend-on-Sea, on the Thames estuary, would not be as it is today. History and cultural heritage is, of course, more complex than this, as the authors of the report note, but I am happy to have this knowledge form a part of my own consciousness and history between these two places.

---

23 'Comparative Analysis of the Landscape and Cultural Heritage of the Wadden Sea Region' (Essex County Council, 2010) p22.

Vlieland, overlooking the North Sea, 2019

PAGLESHAM

Paglesham is one of those places that bears an increasing amount of meaning. When you come from a town (a gaudy seaside town with its crooked houses; its cacophony of seagull cries piercing the drone of cars; its jackpot prizes and 'We've Got a Winner!' arcade jingles carrying in the wind and rattling sailboat masts) travelling anywhere outside of it can feel like a trip to the depths of some forgotten land – the countryside. My memories as a kid of Dad driving us through Rochford, most likely playing 'Ghost Town' by The Specials, and onto the winding roads leading to The Plough and Sail Inn, have created in my mind a recognition. This pub, dating back to the 17th century, with its low ceilings, tiny doors and wooden beams, feels quite far removed from anywhere. It's where I chose to spend my 18th birthday. Years later, I visited with a close friend and we walked along the raised embankment overlooking the River Crouch and Paglesham Creek. We sat on top of one of the old World War II pillboxes and talked about things I can't remember anymore.

Two days before my 26th birthday, I drove there with the

artist Daniel and Clara[24] who was interested in the mysteries of the salt marsh, fish and chips and the Parish Church of St. Peter, situated on a lane fittingly called Old Worlds End. It was the first time I had visited the church, one of the oldest in the area with some 12th-century work and known for its unique, fantastically morbid skull and cross tombstones embedded into the floor inside. The tombstones, probably taken from the churchyard and laid as paving inside the church, date to the late 1600s but are in remarkable condition.

FIELDNOTES: SKULLS BONES STONES
PAGLESHAM CHURCH
20 JAN 2020
DANIEL & CLARA

Fieldnotes, 2020, Daniel and Clara

---

24 I had the pleasure to meet Daniel and Clara, who describe themselves as 'one artist split into two human forms', during an artist's residency at Metal Southend in Chalkwell Hall. Their recent work with the moving image, photography, installation, letters and performance focuses on the British countryside as a site for encounters with the mysterious, the eerie, the otherworldly and the unknown. These two humans were, in other words, the perfect companion to a trip to Paglesham. For more information, visit daniel-clara.co.uk.

Later in the year, my parents and I drove around that area before crossing the Crouch and onto Wallasea Island. The fields were hazy and warm from low-lying cloud. We passed old sheds, rising on stilts and sinking into the salt mud. Paglesham turned out to be the final resting place of HMS *Beagle*, the famous vessel on which Charles Darwin spent a five-year voyage circumnavigating the globe, leading to the formation of his theory of evolution by natural selection, published in his book *On the Origin of Species* in 1859.

HMS *Beagle*, once it had returned from South America, was sold and repurposed to fulfil other work. Such was its fate that it came to the district of Rochford in Essex to be stationed to watch for smugglers who frequently took advantage of the winding creeks and inlets to hide and shift their illegal contraband. HMS *Beagle* was likely dismantled at a ship dock and its pieces sold on. The dock was initially left in the mud to disappear, but ahead of the bicentenary of the vessel's launch in May 2020, the site was excavated and it is now recognised as a scheduled monument with plans for an observation platform to be built overlooking the River Roach. Two hundred years after one of the world's most famous vessels launched, I am able to explore the ship in impressive panoramic vision, from bow to stern, port to starboard.[25] I am able to read the inscription on the wheel – a

---

25 Rochford District Council, with funding from the Heritage Lottery Fund, has launched a CGI Tour of *The Beagle* as part of the Discover 2020 festival to 'commemorate the spirit of adventure in a voyage around Rochford District's rich heritage.' The bicentenary celebration of the ship on Wallasea Island was supposed to commence in May 2020, followed by a multi-form festival of Rochford in June, but was cancelled due to the Coronavirus pandemic.

homage to the battle of Trafalgar – 'England expects every man to do his duty,' and I admit I feel overwhelmed. Overwhelmed by the ability of technology to render in such immense detail something so significant (and I don't necessarily mean its significance to the world of natural sciences and Western scientific thinking); how the ship, its legacy and the disruption it brought to lands that did not ask to be dissected will never be laid to rest.

The discovery is undeniably one of importance and excitement for maritime historians and the local community alike, but it is my feeling that its journey to decay should not have been disrupted. By nature, a vessel will have many purposes in its life. Whether it is to hold some liquid or foodstuff, or if it has been crafted as a cradle to animals or humans, a vessel will undergo changes in direction and in cargo. Why then not let this vessel embark on a final journey rather than serving as some immortal relic of the past? After all, the process of boat decay is a well-practiced and loved ritual within maritime and fishing tradition.

The significance of the discovery, and of HMS *Beagle*'s CGI rendering, should extend beyond what written history has ascribed to it. By that I mean the story of Darwin and his theory of evolution, which has become synonymous with this ship. The voyage that led to Darwin's discoveries should be remembered against the backdrop of colonialism and slavery of the time. As such, we should be open to new ideas about the preservation of contested sites like this and others that Caitlin DeSilvey sets out in her book *Curated Decay: Heritage Beyond Saving* (2017).

Screenshot of HMS *Beagle* CGI Sailing. Bow view

Screenshot of HMS *Beagle* CGI Sailing. The top-left quote reads: 'If the misery of the poor be caused not by the laws of nature, but by our institutions, great is our sin' – Charles Darwin

Screenshot of the HMS *Beagle* CGI Sailing. The top-right quote reads: 'We stopped looking for monsters under our bed when we realised they were inside us' – Charles Darwin

Charles Darwin was outspoken against slavery in his writings in *The Voyage of the Beagle* and it has been argued that this attitude was a catalyst towards his theory of evolution tracing all of human ancestry back to a common origin, as opposed to the belief at the time that white people came from a different and superior race. It is also thought that Darwin's views may have been influenced by John Edmonstone who taught taxidermy at the University of Edinburgh. John Edmonstone was born into slavery in South America and spent his early years on a plantation owned by a Scottish politician named Charles Edmonstone. John was taught how to stuff birds by the naturalist Charles Waterton who would visit the plantation and in 1817 John was granted freedom after travelling to Glasgow with his owner. The skills that John had learnt in Demerara were later passed on to Darwin; skills that Darwin needed in order to secure his position on HMS *Beagle* and to develop his theory of evolution. Legal history, by way of written record, tells us that John Edmonstone died a free man. However, Edmonstone would have had to endure the effects of enslavement and the racist beliefs and actions of the time throughout his life. But it is Charles Darwin's name that we are taught in classrooms, despite Edmonstone playing a fundamental role in the development of Darwin's ideas. HMS *Beagle*, this proclaimed noble vessel of knowledge, travelled to foreign lands taking colonisers and bringing back the colonised. The captain of HMS *Beagle*, Captain Robert Fitzroy, abducted a native Yámana Indian, given the name Jemmy Button as a reminder of the price paid for him – a few buttons from the Captain's coat – and brought him back to England to try to civilise him before returning him to his indigenous land as 'enlightened'. This is described in *The Voyage of the Beagle* and retold in Sylvia Iparraguirre's novel of historical fiction *Tierra del Fuego*. Like all famed British history, the ship's legacy is not all it seems to be. In the words of Iparraguirre's protagonist, 'England has hardly ever cared disinterestedly about the world existing behind the facts.'[26]

Back in Paglesham, the mud dock where the dismantled ship bore out its final days has become a maritime relic, a symbol that ascribes meaning to the regional area and a physically (and digitally) protected, national site. At the announcement of its status as a scheduled monument, Nigel Huddleston, Heritage Minister, said: 'As 2020 marks a special anniversary in the *Beagle*'s past, it is fitting that the significant site of its last days will be protected for the future.' But should HMS *Beagle*'s past

---

26 Sylvia Iparraguirre, translated by Hardie St. Martin, *Tierra del Fuego* (Curbstone Press, 2000) p36.

be preserved in a way that it is permanently enshrined in the landscape? Can it not be said that the ship's legacy lives through the living status of the work carried out by the people who sailed it, and if so, should the ship not be allowed to follow its final course? I am not a heritage expert (I am an expert in nothing) and my opinion, I have no doubt, is an unpopular one, but I would have preferred to learn that, despite its recognition, the remains of the berth were left to collapse into the Paglesham salt marsh, along with any remnants of the ship.

Paglesham, January 2020

Under the hills of Hadleigh Castle sits Two Tree Island, a 10-mile drive south-west of Paglesham and just off from Leigh-on-Sea and the old fishing village Old Leigh. If you keep your eye out on the walk to Two Tree Island, via the path from Leigh-on-Sea railway station, you may be able to see the wreck of the *Souvenir* – a 40-foot, 12-tonne Thames Bawley fishing boat – nesting in the mud. This boat represents the Graveyard of Lost Species project, a temporary monument created by artists YoHa and Critical Art Ensemble. The project celebrates the local tradition of wrecking boats on the salt marsh which in turn act as a concrete but decaying memory of what has passed. Laser-carved onto the boat are the names of various 'lost species' – wildlife, marine creatures, people, livelihoods, fishing methods, landmarks, mythologies, and local dialects that once flourished in the Thames Estuary and are now absent.

In a conversation on the *Souvenir* between Graham Harwood, Rachel Lichtenstein, Steve Barnes and Steve Kurtz of Critical Art Ensemble, I was taken by Steve Kurtz speaking about their work on 'anti-monuments'. The following passage is an excerpt of the transcript and it is what I will think about on the day I stand on the newly constructed observational viewing platform in Paglesham, as I hold my smartphone up to the horizon and walk the *Beagle*'s decks in CGI.

'How do you make a monument that, rather than creating a smooth ideological space in which all people are expected to feel and believe in the same way, how do you do one instead that accounts for difference and allows for the contradictions and conflict of history, and to let all those different voices speak out? And so that was kind of the project we wanted to make, because the voices are all different; it might be a community but there's not unity of story, the stories do not all go together, there are vastly different interpretations of what's going on, and how do you accommodate all of those interpretations? [...] They will be inscribed into this boat. We wanted to do the opposite of the general monument, in which normally you start with a big chunk of stone, and you go "this is gonna last forever", and we're going the exact opposite, it's like let's use some really precarious material and object that's going to come apart, just like our memories, to try to align it with real subjective memory which is fragile and disappears and changes over time. And that's what this boat will do once we inscribe it with these stories and put it back out on the marsh; instead of being an oppressive giant stone to bother people for the next thousand years, it will be an ever-changing series of narratives that will decompose over time.'[27]

This process of allowing the physical object, stories and memories to evolve and change over time, rather than fixing them to a custodial, permanent place, is something that the scholar Caitlin DeSilvey has written about extensively and whose thinking I look to as a source of new ideas when it comes to finding progress in decay.

---

27 Extract from film 'Graveyard of Lost Species-In Conversation: Graham Harwood, Rachel Lichtenstein and Critical Art Ensemble #1' © James Ravinet, quoting Steve Kurtz as part of *Wrecked on the Intertidal Zone*, a project commissioned by Arts Catalyst (2015).

Two Tree Island

MARRUM

An opportunistic, random positioning of windmills in the field of vision of this monument is the death blow to its rare artistic quality. If I were Ids, I'd blow them up.

It tempeltsje op'e dyk (*The Dyke Temple*) by Frisian artist Ids Willemsma has sat on the sea wall in Marrum, north of Leeuwarden in Friesland (a Northern province of the Netherlands) since 1993. Three years later, nine wind turbines were installed in an effort to meet a wind energy quota of 200 megawatts by the millennium. These new Dutch windmills were erected about 600 metres away from Willemsma's Dyke Temple; a 400 tonne structure with 12 poles that measure to the height of the old sea dyke (and which represent the 12 provinces of the Netherlands) that lift up a clay soil roof to the level of the new dyke. The original grass roof is 100 square metres in the shape and size of the old sea dyke.

In an article from 1996 in the Dutch daily newspaper *De Volkskrant*, Rudi Fuchs, then director of the Stedelijk Museum in Amsterdam, zealously defends the sculpture and the surrounding dyke from the proposed further 300 turbines: 'From the Wadden Sea, the Frisian coast will soon look like one big pincushion'.[28] True, though I can't help but think that if Willemsma's sculpture was turned on its head, it too would resemble a pincushion.

I also think that there is nothing more telling of the Dutch mentality, and of humanity itself perhaps, than of Fuchs' hypothetical suggestion that if he were the artist, he'd blow up the turbines. There must be autonomy over one's own work, and whether the threat be barbarous civil servants and politicians, as Willemsma once had them described, or inundating sea water, the power of man, and later of technology, triumphs over that which attempts to thwart them. As the saying goes, God created the world, but the Dutch created the Netherlands.

The Netherlands as it is now has been in a process of formation since the end of the last ice age, 11,700 years ago. Aside from changes in the four main natural processes that have formed the Netherlands – relative sea-level rise, the tide and waves, river dynamics and peat formation – it is humans who have contributed to the largest changes in the landscape. The first major changes came from the increase in population and infrastructure during the Roman period, along with the native population who had begun to cultivate naturally draining peatlands which caused peat to oxidise, compact and flood. Research has shown that in Friesland, and especially Zeeland, 'the decomposition of the peatlands through human intervention was so extensive that the sea was able to create openings in the coast and to gain a hold on the hinterland.

---

28 Wio Joustra, 'Kunstenaar Ids Willemsma verzet zich tegen aantasting van zijn werk 'Dijktempel' ontluisterd door windturbines' (*De Volkskrant*, 1996).

Consequently, at high tide and during storm surges large areas were lost in a very short time. Unwittingly, people had caused major damage to the landscape.'[29]

Time passed and landscape and society returned to an earlier state.

The exploitation of peatlands continued once again as more land was colonised to support new demographic growth when the area of the present-day Netherlands joined the Carolingian empire. The hydrological issues that came with reclaiming peatland were this time overcome by technology such as the famous Dutch windmills, an early 15th-century design which travelled across the North Sea so that soon windmills would be emerging out of a waterlogged Essex landscape too. However, the raised embankments formed by the windmills that drained water from the polders when the water levels were high, created a new problem in preventing seawater from flowing freely across the land during floods and storm surges:

'The decline of the storm surge storage capacity of the marshes induced a dangerous increase of the storm flood levels at the seaward side of the dykes. When a dyke was breached, the water would flood the land behind it, engulfing people and livestock and causing long-term damage. Dyke breaches are not natural disasters!'[30]

---

29 Peter Vos, Michiel van der Muelen, Henk Weerts and Jos Bazlemans (eds), *Atlas of the Holocene Netherlands: Landscape and Habitation since the Last Ice Age* (Amsterdam University Press, 2020) p27-28.
30 Ibid.

The colonisation of land in the Netherlands and the power that humans wielded during times of animal, wind, and later in the 19th and 20th centuries, fossil fuel power, has proven to be a double-edged sword. It has allowed them to shape their country, sustain themselves from the sea, but often at the expense of everything they have tried to create and protect.[31]

Like all temples, Willemsma's is a spatial work that demands a certain expectation of how it should be attended to, viewed and appreciated. The wind turbines posed a threat to his vision: 'It is most effective when there are no disturbances from buildings,' he writes in an explanation to his 'homage to the dyke builder who has raised the ground for centuries to protect humans and animals against the incalculable sea'. For Rudi Fuchs it is 'as in the old tradition, a triumphator raised by his men in a battle'. The artwork is further described as 'magnetic' and it is argued that, in its ideal positioning and intended impact, the viewer involuntarily sees the temple and forces, of nature or of by art, force you to wonder at 'the grandeur of this place, the encounter of nature and culture, the mudflats and the polder'.[32] What is interesting about the debate between this group

---

31 The entire province of Flevoland, measuring 550 square metres, was created in 1986 out of the inland Zuiderzee (South Sea) and is entirely below sea level. The fishing village of Urk was historically an island settlement in the middle of the Ijsselmeer that became the Zuiderzee in the 13th century. Today, it is a coastal village and home to a moving fisherman memorial, looking out to the sea. The province is sustained by dykes and wind-powered electric pumps but continues to drop as it dries out.
32 Wio Joustra, 'Kunstenaar Ids Willemsma verzet zich tegen aantasting van zijn werk 'Dijktempel' ontluisterd door windturbines' (*De Volkskrant*, 1996).

of artists, curators and councillors is that it is about the contradictions that lie within landscape, aesthetics and monuments. While the Provincial Executive of Friesland admitted that there may have been 'a negative influence on the aesthetic values of the artwork', they also explain their belief that the art is safeguarded precisely because of the other spatial elements surrounding (and therefore a part of) the Temple: 'We do not always experience this area as a completely open landscape. There are several ascending elements such as agricultural buildings, groups of trees and bushes, a single windmill or tower silo on a farmyard.' However, the final word in the 1993 article in *De Volkskrant* is given to Rudi Fuchs:

'The statue is a lonely, but watchful watchman. Windmills would make the image appear small, destroying everything it wants and needs to express. The work of art then becomes meaningless.'[33]

I visited the Dyke Temple on a bright but windy day. The wind carried the cold. I was struck by the activity of the place, despite its rural location. The Temple itself is an immense solid structure and the black metal beams lifting up the old dyke are of a spaceship-like architecture; I think it would not look out of place on the set of a science fiction film. Everything where the Temple stands is moving. On the roof, grass and weeds from the old dyke, held high, are flung back and forth in the wind. The floodplain overlooked by the Temple is inhabited by hundreds of birds you can't really hear because the wind,

33 Wio Joustra, 'Kunstenaar Ids Willemsma verzet zich tegen aantasting van zijn werk 'Dijktempel' ontluisterd door windturbines' (*De Volkskrant*, 1996).

unobstructed, charges about the flat land, lifting up the birds like a swarm. The sheep are on the move. The windmills are constantly, invisibly, churning up the wind. They are placed in the land on the side of the Temple where the narrow gravel road leading up to it is. They do not strike me as obtrusive but indeed play a part in the unexpected cacophony of the place.

The Dyke Temple

The floodplain

Three windmills

Willemsma's *Dyke Temple* can be seen as part of a wider maritime memory landscape. The material used to make the sculpture constitutes the clay and grass from the old dyke; in this sense it is a relic of a structure built to protect people from the sea. In his work on maritime death, memory and landscape from the North Sea coast and islands, Norbert Fischer defines maritime relics and memorials to both describe and reflect on the regional past. The objects appear along the coast in such density that they can be seen as a 'memory landscape':

'A social consensus has been established about the symbolic meaning of relics concerning maritime disasters as a self-interpretation of the region's past and culture, and thus can be seen as a symbolic condensation of the tragic past and as part of the cultural heritage of the coast.' [34]

In his anthropomorphism of the object *The Dyke Temple* as a 'lonely watchman', Fuchs shows just how highly symbolised such relics are along coastlines and tidal rivers. 'The extreme landscape of the North Sea coast and social identity are here in a narrow, even indissoluble relationship: floods play a decisive role in collective consciousness.' [35] The protection that the dykes offer Marrum against the North Sea and risk of flooding charges Willemsma's *Temple* with meaning: 'Dealing with water is the decisive element in the understanding of regional history.' For Fischer, such maritime memory landscapes make these places 'hydrographic' societies, a term applied to the

---

34 Norbert Fischer, 'Maritime Death, Memory and Landscape' in *Waddenland Outstanding* (Amsterdam University Press, 2018) p170.
35 Ibid p173.

Netherlands of the 17th century by the historian Simon Schama. They are defined by their interaction with the water.

The image of *The Dyke Temple* is the album artwork for a record titled *Youth Hunt* (2017) by the Dutch band The Homesick. The musicians Elias Elgersma, Jaap van der Velde and Erik Woudwijk are from Dokkum, Friesland, about 16km east of Marrum and 30km east of Zwarte Haan: 'The start of the world' and the place where I began to learn how to site my homesickness in relation to the Frisian landscape. I was introduced to the music of The Homesick within my first year of living in the Netherlands, the same year that *Youth Hunt* was released. Aside from the fact that the band makes excellent music, and without wanting to overly ascribe meaning to coincidence, from the year of the album's release to the band's name, this album instils a sense of inexhaustible longing – it has somewhat become a soundtrack to my experience of the Dutch landscape.

The Netherlands and homesickness belong to one another. Landscapes, as Christopher Tilley and Kate Cameron-Daum suggest, are inexhaustible and unbounded; rhizomic rather than rooted.[36] This is my experience: being homesick or having the affliction of homesickness is to be unrooted, to be neither here nor there. I moved to a country where the landscape might be deemed as unrooted. Is it the unknowing of how the land lies in relation to water? The constant shift of land that is taken and then taken back. Or is it actually a false sense of stability, of control, the victory of humans, to put land under our own feet.

---

36 Christopher Tilley and Kate Cameron-Daum, 'The anthropology of landscape, materiality, embodiment, contestation and emotion' in *An Anthropology of Landscape* (UCL Press, 2017) p1.

False because we do not know how long it will stay there.

'St. Boniface,' my favourite song from *Youth Hunt*, stirs the sensation of clambering over castle ruins, weather-beaten, estuarial. History, especially local history, is defining despite being hard to define. Hundreds, even thousands of years, feels like ancient history to most, though of course, the age of humanity is nothing in comparison to the age of the Earth. Each pair of hands, soft soles of trainers, stubbed out cigarettes, carved names and dates that have left a mark on the ruins of Hadleigh Castle in Essex are what bind humans to history. Charlie Gere writes, 'Perhaps every landscape can be seen inscribed by the endless passionate and violent processes through which it bears witness to what it has endured, whether meteorological, geological, biological or human, but it is the human inscription that binds such a landscape to language and thus to history and the human.'[37] The 8th-century Christian martyr Saint Boniface was an Anglo-Saxon missionary, born as Wynfrid into a noble Wessex family. Consecrated as a missionary bishop and renamed Boniface by Pope Gregory II in Rome, his mission was to spread Christianity in the pagan Frankish kingdom. Boniface was killed by pagan Frisians as he was preaching on the 5th of June in 754 in Dokkum, the provincial hometown of The Homesick – it is a part of the band's heritage.

Historical monuments such as those of Saint Boniface in Dokkum and indeed the monument of the Saint in the form of a song written and performed by The Homesick are

---

37 Charlie Gere, *I Hate the Lake District* (Goldsmiths Press, 2019) p52-53.

manifestations of a memory landscape. The metaphor I used of describing listening to 'St. Boniface' as clambering over the ruins of Hadleigh Castle constitutes a part of my local memory landscape. All through the summer, dog-walkers, teenagers, families walk to Hadleigh Castle as a sort of local ritual. The ruins of which, and they really are ruins, are heralded as ancient markers that stand stoically as an indication of our collective past and heritage.[38]

When people visit the ruins and set down their picnic blankets, or sit to sketch the ruins, or crack open their cans of warming beer, or take photos of the ruins and of each another, where do they situate themselves? Is it within the history of the place? Or is it within the local identity? Of course, most enjoying a day out at Hadleigh Castle are probably thinking of neither but certainly there is a strong sense of regional identity in Southend. A visit to the ruins remains to be one of the activities considered as a

---

38 I use the word 'ancient' inasmuch as perceived history is subjective. The stones are not from ancient history in the technical sense but may be perceived as ancient by children, for example, who have a lesser understanding of the general timeline of human history, or for adults or elders who may well remember climbing the ruins when they were children, a lifetime ago, ancient history. In fact, the beginnings of the castle were built around 1215 and were refortified during the Hundred Years War, though the site was of strategic importance well before this period. At the site of Hadleigh Castle, thereabouts, the Danes occupied a fortified camp with ships moored in the waters below where the ruins of the castle now stand. In AD 894 during the struggles between the Saxons and the Danes, the Battle of Beamfleote (Benfleet, Essex) took place at this site where the Saxon army led by King Alfred the Great came from London and stormed the fort and the Danes gave up the land. A year later, a wooden church was built on the site of the Battle. The church that stands there now was built on the foundations of the Saxon church.

rite of passage if you live there or nearby.[39]

The formation of the (maritime) memory landscape, according to Fischer, actually begins mostly after the mid-19th century, a period of social upheaval and identity. The expansion of seaside resorts demanded self-assurance of identity within coastal and island communities, yet the loss of political autonomy as tourism and state influence grew, fuelled the fear of a loss of identity.[40] Southend and places like Canvey Island underwent this crisis of identity after being developed in the 19th century as seaside resorts and experiencing a decline in the 1960s onwards. This fluctuation of identity along with its proximity to and permeable relationship with East London, historically one of the poorest areas of the capital, are distinctive elements of the development of Essex. One of the main examples that constitute a maritime memory landscape for Fischer, is that of flood marks in remembrance of storm surges and flooding. These are found in many harbour towns and coastal resorts.[41] They can be in the form of lines indicating the flood level against a wall, such as that in the fishing village Old Leigh and the Foulness Island Heritage Centre to mark the flood

---

39 Southend is technically a borough and comprises the towns of Chalkwell, Eastwood, Essex, Leigh-on-Sea, North Shoebury, Prittlewell, Shoeburyness, Southchurch, Thorpe Bay, and Westcliff-on-Sea. Hadleigh Castle is situated between Leigh-on-Sea and Benfleet and can be accessed from the town of Hadleigh or Leigh.
40 Norbert Fischer, 'Maritime Death, Memory and Landscape' in *Waddenland Outstanding* (Amsterdam University Press, 2018) p171.
41 Fischer writes that some of these markers are particularly integrated into the coastal landscape, like the flood level indicators on the river Weser promenade of Bremerhaven, in the sea resorts of St. Peter Ording and on the beach of Dangast (Jadebusen), one of the first sea resorts on the German North Sea coast.

of 1953, or that in Groningen in the Netherlands that marks a deadly flood from 26 January 1682. I believe they can also be the less obvious markers found in flooded houses, hidden behind wallpaper or through damaged household items, through the absence of lost photographs.

1953 flood level marker, Old Leigh, Essex

CANVEY ISLAND

CANVEY ISLAND

...and slimy stakes stuck out of the mud, and slimy stones stuck out
of the mud, and red landmarks and tidemarks stuck out of the mud,
and an old landing-stage and an old roofless building slipped into
the mud, and all about us was stagnation and mud.[42]

CHARLES DICKENS, GREAT EXPECTATIONS

A low-level world made and remade. When you look at a map and
at the point in which the North Sea basin narrows, you'll see the
markings of an island called Canvey. Take your finger and trace
it across the water and you'll disembark roughly at Middelburg
in the Zeeland province of the Netherlands. This is significant
to the many floods the two places have had to endure together
over history. How much do lines tell us? Do floodlines, those
marked on walls to indicate the ghost of a watery disaster, make

---

42 Charles Dickens travelling out of London towards the mouth of the
estuary in chapter 54 of *Great Expectations*. Dickens' description of the
navigation and tides taken to go 'where the river is broad and solitary,
where the waterside inhabitants are very few, and where lone public-
houses are scattered here and there, of which we could choose one for
a resting-place'. The causeway outside the inn where they arrive to is
thought to be by The Lobster Smack, Canvey Island.

us more aware of the memory, history and commemoration of place? Or are they too fixed, providing only a static reminder of an event so dynamic? Norbert Fischer describes flood marks as narratives of a very specific regional history. They are symbolic sites of maritime death. Through such sites, the history of the coast is inscribed into the landscape.[43]

Even in the case of lines drawn by your finger across a map, connecting two places of significance to one another, do these give away as much as words? Words with their hard and their soft edges, how they rise and fall out of mouths.

Floods have recurrently torn apart the islands, inlets and creeks around the Essex estuary. The land here is unconsolidated and continually in movement. In 1969, P.A. and D.P. Arnold, on behalf of the Foulness Island Residents Committee, prepared a neat little pamphlet entitled 'FOULNESS', after the largest of the Essex islands. In it, they detail some of the floods recorded in these areas: from AD 31, when Romans had to abandon their coastal settlements and evacuate to Shoeburyness, then known as Essobiria; to 1099 when it was recorded 'the sea flood sprung to such a height and did so much harm as no man remembered that it ever did before; then to 1236 (another town lost, over 100 dead); and so it goes on.[44] On to the 17th century when flooding continued and:

---

43 Norbert Fischer, 'Maritime Death, Memory and Landscape' in *Waddenland Outstanding* (Amsterdam University Press, 2018) p169.
44 P.A. and D.P. Arnold on behalf of the Foulness Island Residents Committee, FOULNESS (1969) p2.

'The little isles of Candy [Canvey] and Fowlnesse [Foulness] on the coast of Essex were quite under water, not a hoof was saved thereon, and the inhabitants were taken from the upper parts of their houses into boats.'

Despite the doomed geological composition of the land, in the same century it was decided that the sodden landmass overlooked by the Hadleigh marshes, overlooking the estuary and the Nore sandbank, was worthy. As the money poured in so the water drained out. Thus, Canvey was born. At this point the Dutch were already renowned for their technological innovation in water management. Dutch engineer Joas Croppenburgh was contracted to drain and reclaim the land, allowing the owners not only to save it, but also to monetise it. Croppenburgh was to 'inn, gain and recover from the inundacion and overflowing on the river of Thames' 3,600 acres on the island, nearly 1,500 of which were owned by Sir Henry Appleton of South Benfleet. It has been traditionalised that Cornelius Vermuyden was the Dutch engineer to carry out the 'inning', but Hilda Grieve has found no stronger evidence for this other than 'Croppenburgh's marriage with Vermuyden's great-niece, and a reference in 1626 to Vermuyden's having "assisted" him with another contract to close the "great breach" at Erith in Kent.'[45] But echoes remain of the Dutch families employed by Croppenburgh who settled on Canvey Island, most notably the two Dutch octagonal cottages. One of them, maintained by the council, dates to 1618.

---

45 Hilda Grieve, *The Great Tide* (Essex County Council, 1959) p25.

Dutch Cottage, Canvey Island

Canvey's Coney Island

CANVEY IS ENGLANDS LOURDES[46]

Oh, great Canvey, island of our dreamscape. Our Candy. Our Coney. Our Venice.

Simultaneously a site of potential and of destruction: from salt marsh, to just-dry land, to oil and gas, returned to water, to land. Oh, land of pirates, of fizz and booty.
Canweye, Canefe, Kaneweye, Kaneveye, Koneveye.[47]

Our father, Frederick Hester, looking to Allhallows, builds in his mind a utopia. Puts his money where his mouth is and watches a kingdom dissolve. The beginnings of a dream are the most unreachable, yet are the formations of the stage that

---

46 *CANVEY IS ENGLANDS LOURDES*. Words from a mural painted on Canvey Island's sea wall in 1985. Restored in 2017 by Friends of Concord Beach. The mural is believed to pay homage to Nora Arthurs, a practicing Catholic who moved from London to Roggel Road in the 1940s. Arthurs was known to have visions and built a shrine of the Virgin Mary in her back garden. Her house came to be known as 'Mary's House'. The Friends believe Catholics from around the world made pilgrimages to the shrine in Mrs Arthur's garden, as they do similarly to Lourdes in southwest France. A spokesman for the Friends explained: 'Cheaper air travel in the 1960s to 1980s meant many pilgrims could travel on pilgrimage to Lourdes in France – some in the hope of miraculous cures. Pilgrims came from all around the world to Canvey and it is thought one was responsible for the message "Canvey is Englands Lourdes" painted on the seawall.' From an article by Chloe Chapman in the *Southend Echo*, 2017.
47 One of the many names previously given to Canvey Island. From: 'A blizzard of ashes: notes on *CANWEYE {   }*', Ellen Greig, 2016.

we step onto; the threads that make up the lush moss-green curtains and the soft bridges beneath our feet. By the time we reach the latter part of our dream and the script is played out, the set crumbles and our mind's early designs are reduced to rubble. What manner of theatre is the dream, asks Sebald, in which we are at once playwright, actor, stage manager, scene painter and audience?[48]

> *Canweye is a script unto itself, a flat page of*
> *landscape that could be read.*[49]

Frederick Hester's 20th-century dream to develop the wetlands of Canvey into a holiday resort (piers, gardens and walkways carved out in the mud like worm tracks) is one of the most strange and beautiful stories of childlike imagination that I have come across. His ambition was to build a little Venice, complete with its own Grand Canal and Essex Rialto Bridge. A little Venice with Dutch flourishes.

> *On every new thing there lies already the*
> *shadow of annihilation.*[50]

Like Giethoorn in the Netherlands, the Venice of Holland, tourism is the flood. Like Venice, tourism is the annihilator. Canvey's champagne lands, sold cheap to investors and holidaymakers, became the flood. One way that Hester would try to sell his Venetian Island dream was to decorate it Dutch – a nod to the men Hester considered as fathers of the island.

---

48 W.G. Sebald, *The Rings of Saturn* (New Directions, 1979) p79-80.
49 Frances Scott, script for *CANWEYE {   }* (Focal Point Gallery, 2016).
50 W.G. Sebald, *The Rings of Saturn* (New Directions, 1979) p24.

Twentieth-century dreamer Frederick Hester envisioned refurbishing the island into a fantastical Essex Venice. The land was cheap and close to London and could have been the product of a centuries old symbiotic relationship between the two places. But as Gillian Darley observes in her contribution to the project *Radical Essex*,[51] by the late-19th century the push and pull between East London and Essex had reached a crisis point. The development of the 'Bungalow Town' of Lea Bridge was one solution to the overflow from the housing crisis in London. The opening of the Lea Bridge railway station in 1840 which brought water and gas to the area also paved the way for the development of 70 'shacks' close to the railway track. Darley notes that it was this initiative that drove those who became known as 'plotlanders' in the next generation. Darley writes: 'In the early 1920s the pre-war trickle became a flood. Potential purchasers, lured out of London to attend the auctions with free rail tickets and a lavish meal ... might need to buy two or three adjacent plots in order to secure enough ground."[52] A lavish meal possibly with champagne. I imagine Hester, sitting opposite his companion in the train carriage, drawing up plans and drinking, sealing the deal and selling off saltmarsh to holidaymakers looking to escape the East End. That is why they call it the champagne lands, sodden and fizzy with life.

The plots were developed around rudimentary dwellings that

---

51 Radical Essex is a project re-examining the county in relation to radicalism in thought, lifestyle, politics and architecture, shedding light on the vibrant, pioneering thinking of the late-19th and 20th centuries.
52 Gillian Darley, 'From Plotlands to New Towns' in Radical Essex (Focal Point Gallery, 2018) 104.

were often little more than sheds. These created what Darley calls a 'domestic bricolage'[53], caught between the owners' desire to create a home and to protect themselves from the weather. The early shacks on Canvey Island were 'encrusted with turrets, bound by verandas and trelliswork and topped by weathervanes.'[54] To this day, these individualistic qualities remain and there are striking variations in the houses, the road names, and the everyday objects the inhabitants have used to make their homes.

Chris Fenwick is manager of Dr Feelgood, the Canvey R&B and pub-rock band perhaps most famous for its 1979 hit 'Milk and Alcohol'. On a walking tour with him, Chris told me that the

---

53 I first heard the term 'bricolage' in a seminar on William Blake during my undergraduate degree. It is used by the anthropologist Claude Lévi-Strauss to describe the process of creating something useful out of the discarded parts of life. Jon Mee, in his book *Dangerous Enthusiasm: William Blake and the Culture of Radicalism in the 1790s* (1994), uses the notion of 'bricolage' to argue that the political radicalism of Blake's work is more significant than was previously thought. Levi-Strauss writes in *The Savage Mind* that 'mythical thought ... builds ideological castles out of the debris of what was once a social discourse.' For Mee, Blake's complex political perspective was directly involved with the discourse of radicalism in the 1790s during the French Revolution. This was of particular interest to what I was working on at the time, asking how the work of William Blake on the imagination informs our reading of contemporary socio-political theory on framed identity as outlined in Judith Butler's *Frames of War*. 'The frame is always throwing something away, always keeping something out, always de-realizing and de-legitimating alternative versions of reality, discarded negatives of the official version. And so, when the frame jettisons certain versions of war, it is busily making a rubbish heap whose animated debris provides the potential resources for resistance.' Judith Butler, *Frames of War: When is Life Grievable?* (Verso, 2010) XIII.
54 Gillian Darley, 'From Plotlands to New Towns' in *Radical Essex* (Focal Point Gallery, 2018) p103.

houses are all different because there are so many housing contractors. Chris was born in 1953 and like many born in the year of the flood was called a 'flood baby'. The son of a house builder, he can tell you just by looking at a house the company that designed and built it. I was able to meet Chris during a walk around the site of Canvey Wick. With the wind whipping up the sea, it's difficult to imagine the absence of the concrete sea wall that's in place now. At the time of the 1953 flood, there was no such wall to speak of, just a raised grass mound with a sinking dyke behind. The site of Canvey Wick, with its snaking pier and skeletal remains of the Occidental Oil Refinery, built and shelved in the 1970s before it was ever in use, is now recognised as one of the most biodiverse areas in the UK. It was the stimulus for artist David Blandy's film commission, exhibition and table-top roleplay game *The World After*, which was exhibited at Focal Point Gallery in Southend-on-Sea in 2020. The gallery also organised the walking tour. This took place on a windy and freezing day in January 2020 – conditions I imagine not so dissimilar to that of January 1953. At the end of the walk we reached The Lobster Smack Inn, formerly The Sluice Inn and The World's End. Places with names like The World's End always carry significance. So remote was this area in the 17th and 18th centuries that the public house was a lifeline for mariners heading up the estuary towards London, or in the other direction. Chris tells me that the pub had a mariner's license meaning that anyone travelling by barge, boat or other craft could arrive at any time of the night, bang on the door and be given a jug of ale and some ham, such was the legal duty of the pub.

Dutch eel boats in Canvey's East Haven Creek c1904. Published in the *Nieuwe Harlingen Courant*, 14 October 1932

The Lobster Smack was a place where Dutch fishermen, coming from the Wadden Island of Texel, would stay on their way to Billingsgate Market – their barges-bellies full of live eels. This trade began in the mid-15th century and continued through the 17th century, despite a brief hiatus during the Anglo-Dutch wars. It lasted into to the 1900s when eels were an established street food, particularly in East London where the dish of jellied eels originated.

At the start of the 1970s, Dr Feelgood were frequently playing in pubs on Canvey Island and around the South Essex area, from their regular haunt The Admiral Jellicoe pub on Canvey to The Railway at Pitsea. Chris describes the pub scene on Canvey, and along the seafront in Southend, as deadly. He recalls to me that someone once rode into the Jellicoe on a horse like it was the Wild West.

In the award-winning documentary about Dr Feelgood, *Oil City Confidential* (directed by Julien Temple, 2010), the band's co-founder and lead singer Lee Brilleaux describes Canvey Island as the Thames Delta: 'It could be anywhere... all dressed up but destined to sink.'[55] The film shows a childhood map of Canvey drawn by Brilleaux, with an island in the centre, surrounded by ocean. As children, Canvey was to Lee Brilleaux, Wilko Johnson, John Sparks, John Martin and Chris Fenwick, a place where they could become pirates. Later, as a band, the mudflats, creeks and inlets of the Thames estuary could have been a place where Muddy Waters played. Wilko Johnson, a lover of English literature, is drawn in by Canvey's Miltonic flames.

The proposed Occidental Refinery was abandoned in 1975 but gas works are still in operation on Canvey Island, which imports, stores and exports liquid petroleum gases. Local residents have experienced surprising upsides to this, once again distinguishing their houses from that of the mainland, connected by two bridges to Benfleet, the A130 and the B1014. Canvey Island was one of the first places in the UK to pilot having its natural gas networks converted to deliver hydrogen, and Canvey residents had their gas appliances refitted, courtesy of the Calor Gas Works.[56]

55 Lee Brilleaux in *Oil City Confidential*, directed by Julien Temple (2010).
56 Paul E. Dodds and Stéphanie Demoullin, 'Conversion of the UK gas system to transport hydrogen' in *International Journal of Hydrogen Energy*, Volume 38, Issue 18 (2013).

Cropenburg Walk

Wessem Road

Helden Avenue

Komberg Crescent

Berg Avenue

Heeswyk Road

Hilversum Way

Laars Avenue

Heideburg Road

Kamerwyk Avenue

Winter and Summer Gardens

Waarden Road

Waalwyk Drive

As she gasps for more air she is reminded that she is below sea level. Venice dissolves into the sinking marshlands of Essex.[57]

Korndyk Avenue

---

57 Ellen Greig, 'A blizzard of ashes: notes on *CANWEYE* {   }', (Focal Point Gallery, 2016).

flood baby

The flood baby dances a different way,
steps to meet a high tide with the wind.

Talks about the spray, the salt spray.
That's obvious. But which way the heavy

waves pull, mark tide times
across your wet palms. That's not obvious.

Strange occurrences are not hard to miss:
dancing when water floods open toe heels.

People die and we can feel it, true.
It is felt most keenly in the days after death.

False houses literally keeling under.

Trumpet scales

I imagined the land for years prior to the placement of my boots sinking inside it. As if my community had already met to plan for my arrival, drinking hot soup around the door of a caravan and arranging topographical clues, like simple language spoken into my fastened ears that has settled inwards.

Come to think. I am changing my habits in recognition of new familiarity, arriving at a meeting place on time and soaked from weather. The way in which the North Sea has reshaped land and the way in which the Dutch have reclaimed land and the way in which the sea will take land back is community.

The reconciled have it in them to experiment. Land commands this prescription. Land is haphazard. Unstable and fertile. Land is flat. It is principled and it is desolate despite its dependence on ecology. Land is low, strewn. Bursting. Land is flooded.

Consumed I am sinking into the mud. I am pulled out by a mysterious walker wearing wool trousers and big brown boots who mumbles about a battle from the early Middle Ages, here where I am sinking, when everything disappears. I smell my fingers which have changed consistency.

Consider the herring. I sat along the banks of the proper centre my legs hanging above the water when I cried stingingly. Of all of loss to come we must not forget the loss of the herring. Herring are humble fish of intricate design that have formed land, countries and entire civilisations. Overfished. Banked.

Low Z

I had the impression we were driving over the moon on a foggy February night. The endless dark drive. Memory submerged in fish stock and brittle frozen prawns, their little arms snapping under the weight of hot water. Pinking. Heavy sky. Leaning. Dancers move nowhere against the rising wind. The start of the long night and the new tide was already tired. The motion of the old tide had forced an impression.

Dead tired. Shoulders
slope into ceramic bathtubs
barely covered, hardly rich.
Lukewarm and limescaly.
Comb out worm paths
in dear children's hair
riddled with mud.

Dear children, this is not what they will teach you in your geography lesson. *How to prepare for bed:*

LESSON I

How to detect changes in the wind
Observe familiar movements. Go to your local cinema.
Tell mum and dad how the film was after.

Depressions
Observe suspension of familial ebb and flows.

Domestic reliance
Observe primitive parental and family animal behaviour.

Realignment
Observe personal response to the unfamiliar. Which songs do you sing, if any?

Low K

Keith was baptised by the jetty. It was announced in the school at morning assembly. The palms of child hands purpled cold and patterned with grit. Maybe it was some sort of offering, appeasement of tumultuous weather, an excuse to bring families together to exchange things, emotional practices: cheap hot dinners in front of TV sets, chitchat, prefabs and have you seen the cat, have you seen what's happened here? Keith was supposed to run the relay before the field – well, you know, you've seen it.

High A

No one could say where the land ended and the sea began. Hundreds of chests of drawers hung wide open. Split silos. Saltwater marshes foaming at the mouth with brackish waste: doorknobs; sodden wallpaper; cattle; ruined card games; bed sheets, spoiled; busted bikes; bloated, floating worms.

I knew the land for years prior to my bones inside it. Decay matters more than life, it is true that in the winter everything has sunk and in the summer everything is sinking. I talk to bird watchers while I roll jelly-green sea glass between my fingers until it is round and frosted enough for my earring collection.

On rewilding

Canvey Island is in a state of constant re-negotiation with water, marshland and its peoples, as with all of the islands of Essex. For this reason, investment in marsh, bog, and soggy land – and waterscapes, in all senses – naturally, emotionally, financially – can never have the outcome so desired by those, humans or otherwise, who alter its state.

Canvey Island's history of reclamation, redevelopment and rewilding stretching from the 16th century through to the 21st century makes it a composite island. The land rises and falls, making it fertile for storytelling, welcoming different peoples, and it is open to multiple interpretations and meanings.

On a biological level, though we can never truly rewild a landscape – as in return it to its pre-human condition – (re) creating healthy environments with natural foods, light, clear air and clean water is beneficial to humans and other animals. The Canvey Wick Nature Reserve, once (Dogger)land, sea and river estuary, to saltmarsh, to oil refinery (constructed only partially, but never used), returns in the 1980s onwards to a site of ultra-rich biodiversity.

How radical is the practice of rewilding landscapes? Rewilding is the process by which human alters landscape to restore it to its natural state, often for environmental values, or to transform its properties into capital, supposedly for social values. The restoration of landscapes, however, for all its apparent redemption, often happens at the expense of the very environments it is operating to enhance, or exploit, or save. For that is what rewilding is – an operation, operating in a continuous narrative.

Hester's vision to turn Canvey into a booming resort for jaded Londoners did not materialise. In an article from the *Nottingham Evening Post* in 1903, advertising the Island's grand designs and presumably placed by Hester, it is written that 'Canvey Island, properly speaking, cannot be described as a seaside or a riverside resort, inasmuch as it is a singular and agreeable admixture of both'. Canvey is a composite land below sea level. Had it not been drained and had nature been allowed to follow its course, the island would be under water. In this sense it may be considered as a contradiction.

In an interview about the project *Monsoon Assemblages* with *Migrant Journal* editor Dámaso Randulfe, Lindsay Bremner remarks: 'One of the real contradictions that emerges in these sites comes from the inability of neoliberal global developers to take these conditions into account, since real estate has always been assumed to be dry land. They are trying to turn a wetland into land by displacing water, without realising that water doesn't just go away.' Agreeing with Randulfe's response that the attempt to striate wetlands has always been a colonial imperative, Bremner remarks that 'unless you can demarcate land, you can't charge revenue for it, it has no value'.[58] Floods

---

58 Lindsay Bremner, 'On Monsoon Assemblages' in *Migrant 3: Flowing Grounds* (Migrant Journal, 2017) p92.

have repeatedly torn apart the islands, inlets and creeks around the Essex estuary. It was the recurrent flooding of Canvey Island that deterred Frederick Hester's investors, leading to bankruptcy in 1905 and the abandonment of his heavenly Canvey Island, with its promenade pier, Venetian canal and Dutch-inspired Winter and Summer Gardens.

Similarities between such designed gardens and neoliberal landscapes have been observed in the book *Flow Country*. As products from the profits of empire and inheritance, 18th century gardens sought to control and shape the environment to provide new experiences for the gentry. The afforestation of the Scottish highlands in the 20th century was in part influenced by aesthetics, tourism and recreation, beginning 'during the Romantic period in the late 18th and early 19th centuries when poets, travellers and naturalists discovered both pleasure and scientific interest in British woods long before ecologists and conservationists in the middle of the 20th century'.[59] William Wordsworth, for example, who, in his admiration of the beauty of the Lake District, effectively mapped the landscape onto the national (upper and middle class) consciousness through his writing, such as his poem 'Daffodils' and his guidebook *A Guide Through the District of the Lakes in the North of England*. In doing so, Wordsworth had turned the region into a national asset so when, in the 1920s, the Forestry Commission bought large areas of land to plant conifer forests it was met with resistance – it did not match the image of Englishness and the ideal Lake District landscape.[60]

---

59 Jan Oosthoek, *Conquering the Highlands: A history of the Afforestation of the Scottish Uplands* (Australian National University E Press, 2013) p95.
60 Ibid p96.

In his book *I Hate the Lake District* Charlie Gere writes that 'the original Romantic vision of the Lakes became something far more sentimental, a kind of fetishisation of the natural scenery as an idyll and an escape from the urban and industrial'.[61]

Let us return to *Flow Country*, to the Scottish uplands, to the Blanket Bog. This piece of fictocriticism by Jasper Coppes and Daniel Lee, published by Publication Studio Glasgow in 2018, is a cinematographic, archaeological and literary exploration of contested sites in the far north of Scotland. It offers, as the book's designers My Bookcase describe, 'a possible way out of the many "transformation-narratives" that tried to exploit or reform this vast terrain.' In the book, they consider the industrialisation of the Flow Country peatlands in the 1980s through the state-subsidised planting of coniferous forests. Can these afforestation initiatives be described as 'creative destruction', ask Coppes and Lee, through their ability to capture the innovation and negative impacts on society and the economy inherent in dynamic economic development?[62] This operation of creative destruction is still ongoing and can be most completely explained with a larger extract:

'Certainly, market forces and privatisation led to the destruction of the peatlands to enable further economic growth, however the true 'Creative Destruction' is actually being undertaken by the RSPB [The Royal Society for the Protection

---

61 Charlie Gere, *I Hate the Lake Distri*ct (Goldsmiths Press, 2019) p5.
62 Jasper Coppes and Daniel Lee, *Flow Country* (Publication Studio Glasgow, 2018) p48.

of Birds] in their programme of deindustrialisation through the deforestation and restoration of the peatlands – change, creation and transformation. In felling the neoliberal forests they are transforming one artefact or commodity into another; bog, to forest-capital, to restored-bog-capital. The latter has more social value, as a 'wilderness area' and bird reserve, but still plays to an agenda. The industrial landscape has been 'absorbed, expanded, refurbished and redeveloped' – part of a larger global post-industrial worldview. This re-wilding has created something new and innovative at the expense of the forest.'[63]

Further north in Denmark, another contested site – Vejen Mose in Jutland, the largest raised bog in Northern Europe – is set to be reflooded to meet new emissions targets. Living peat bogs absorb and trap carbon, whereas drained bogs release carbon dioxide when organic matter trapped for thousands of years breaks down.[64] By reflooding a former peat bog that has been drained and turned into cultivated land, the government will be able to offset their carbon emissions. While some farmers welcome the idea of reflooding their land in the effort to tackle the climate crisis, others like Gill Andersen believe that by pulling up the draining pipes and flooding the land will kill the trees and increase noise pollution: 'Without the trees in front of the nearby motorway, the noise from the traffic will come directly up the hills to us.'[65] Herein lays the central question asked by Coppes and Lee: 'Will the reforesting of barren landscapes, with

---

63 Jasper Coppes and Daniel Lee, *Flow Country* (Publication Studio Glasgow, 2018) p48.
64 Richard Orange, 'Danish farmers divided over plan to flood their lands to cut emissions' (*The Guardian*, 2019).
65 Ibid.

which many countries today redeem their guilt in the face of environmental crisis, foster a re-wilding of our environment? Or should we plant our sense of wilderness in another image, one that does not include the use of woods?'[66]

The use of (moving) image and sound to locate ourselves within an environment can be seen as planting our sense of self and wilderness through visual perception and memory. That we are in perpetual reconfiguration with our surroundings through the interaction of culture, mentality and society means that landscape is not just a representation of, but an element of human life. In her text accompanying filmmaker and photographer Alexandra Leykauf's exhibition *CAPRONA*, Julie Jones (following Jean-Marc Besse) says we must consider landscape in this way if we are to challenge European landscape culture which plays a key role in the constitution of national, even nationalist imagery, as in the naturalisation of colonial enterprises.[67] In other words, it is a colonialist imperative that views landscape as an object to transform. Instead, it should be understood that as humans we live in a reciprocal relationship with the organisms that comprise our environment. In the same way, Jasper Coppes and Daniel Lee describe that 'the production of a film has to be considered in terms of the entanglement and interaction between minerals and chemicals and microorganisms of which we, humans, are one particular emanation.'[68] Rewilding

66 Jasper Coppes and Daniel Lee, *Flow Country* (Publication Studio Glasgow, 2018) p48.

67 Julie Jones, 'A new text by Julie Jones, commissioned to accompany Alexandra Leykauf's exhibition CAPRONA' (Artists' Research Centre 2018).

68 Jasper Coppes and Daniel Lee, *Flow Country* (Publication Studio Glasgow, 2018) p23.

can be thought of as a radical act inasmuch as it is continual process, but should only be considered as such in the context of creative destruction. Whether it is in the form of development, afforestation, reflooding, or sandscaping,[69] we should think more critically about the operation of rewilding and its transformation narratives.

---

69 In an effort to save the Bacton Gas Terminal and the villages of Bacton and Walcott in Norfolk, UK, from coastal erosion, a vast sandscaping project is underway whereby nearly two million cubic metres of sand is being shifted to a stretch of the coast to protect it from the sea. In the article 'Vast sand scheme to protect Norfolk coast' (BBC, 2019), Professor Sue Brooks, Birkbeck, University of London, says: 'With the sandscaping scheme... there has been a shift from hard defending the coast to more of a nature-based solution... [It is] a really radical new way of thinking about shoreline management.' Radical for who? Dr Sally Brown, University of Southampton and University of Bournemouth, says that 'one of the biggest challenges is that we can't keep doing that in places that just protect a few people, or maybe in places where flood risks only affect a few houses.' Shouldn't we be thinking about managed retreat, i.e. to move people away from areas of risk, rather than redesigning a landscape (whether it is a nature-based design or not) to buy time – which is estimated at only 15–20 years of extra protection?

Canvey Island, by The Lobster Smack, 2020

OUWERKERK

OUWERKERK

1,835 doden
\ dead

72,500 evacues \   evacuees

2,000
paarden \
ho   rs
e   s

3,000 beschadigde boerderijen \
damaged farms

200,000 hectare   land   onderwater \
hectares   land   underwater

140,000
stuks
pluimvee \
poultry

materiele schade: ruim 1,5 miljardgulden \
material damage: over 1.5 billion guilders

40,000 beschadigde woningen \
damaged homes

12,000
varkens /
pigs

3,000
verwoeste
        woningen
        \
        destroyed
homes

3,000 schapen /
sheep

I am about to leave England from Folkestone and will soon be underwater. It is like I am saying goodbye to the day: I will see you again soon.

I am in a tunnel under the Thames. No, I am in a tunnel under the North Sea. I am in a tunnel under the paddling pool in our old back garden, surrounded by shells.

Around the time that the sea was crashing through northeast Canvey Island, icy water lapping around table and chair legs, similar scenes were happening across the channel in the Netherlands at a significantly more ruinous level. The Dutch story of the flood extends across the country, across generations and it has leached into the national consciousness. Destroyed dykes, inundated farmland, entire families lost in a single night in villages across the province of Zeeland. It was the biggest peacetime tragedy of recent history that haunted the country like a lost and deadly battle. Floods are an integral part of Dutch history and culture. The oldest reliable records of a disastrous storm and subsequent flood that hit the Netherlands date back to Boxing Day 828, written by the French bishop Prudentius of Troyes and also recorded in the *Annales Xantenses*, a Carolingian historical work. These great tides across time have often been recorded through paintings too. *The Saint Elizabeth's Day Flood, Master of the St Elizabeth Panels*, c. 1490–1495 (unknown artist), on display at the Rijksmuseum in Amsterdam, depicts one such flood that occurred in the night of 18-19th November 1421. A heavy northwesterly storm and tidal surge are thought to have caused the flood. More than 20 villages drowned and thousands lost their lives. The city of Dordrecht, which is depicted in the painting, and its surrounding areas were worst affected. At the lowest inland point that the sea reached, the flood water still remains today.

Where does water go when a flood hits land? A lot of it is pumped out or drained to reduce the risk of contamination from sewerage and other pollutants.[70] But some goes on existing: from its furthest reach on its night of entry and from its tidal re-entry through gaps in broken dykes, it seeps into the land for years after, joining a communicative network of waterways across the land. Thus inhabitants of flood-prone areas live alongside that which has destroyed their communities as it is rebuilt and shaped around the flood water.

---

70 On Canvey Island there was a clean-up operation involving 400-800 people on just one weekend. The scene was described as 'not just wet, but contaminated'.

The storm that hit the east coast of the UK and the west coast of the Netherlands followed the same weather trajectory. A northwesterly gale, born on the 29th of January someplace in the Atlantic Ocean, had turned into a hurricane by the time it reached the east coast of Scotland. The continual dance between polar air and equatorial air, where they meet in the northern hemisphere, caused a series of depressions across three days. This is not unusual, but when the depression 'LOW Z' met with the depression 'LOW K', the pressure at the centre dropped and continued to drop throughout the night of Thursday the 29th of January and throughout the whole of Friday the 30th of January. By Friday evening, a southwesterly wind, pushing water from the North Sea south to north, met with a west-northwesterly wind that was pushing water from the Atlantic towards the North Sea. Across Saturday the 31st of January the depression deepened and moved into the North Sea. The furious northwesterly winds, the most dangerous direction for a storm tide, had been forcing water from the Atlantic and effectively funnelling it into the North Sea basin. This icy water would soon meet between England's east coast and the lowlands of the Netherlands.

Over the course of that day the tide barely ebbed on the east coast of England. It did not ebb at all in the Netherlands. At its peak, the storm surge, coinciding with a spring tide,[71] had increased the sea level by four metres in Zeeland (approximately 13 feet). The collapse of the dyke system in the Delta region occurred over a period of 36 hours – from the high tide in the early hours of the 1st of February, with waves of over five metres

71 A spring tide refers not to the season in which the tide is occurring but to its range; a spring tide contains the largest range (think of something being pulled back and springing forward).

(nearly 16.5 feet) beating the sand and clay and forcing gaps in the dykes, through to the devastating second flood tide when the water started to flow through, submerge the polders and completely destroy the dyke, so that even when the storm abated, the normal tides would pour in twice each day, further opening the great wounds.

There is a sense of spectatorship in writing about disasters that you haven't experienced. At times I have felt myself deviate from the flood. The way a meandering river weaves to and fro from each bend to bank. At times it feels as if I'm standing there and the water comes towards me, close enough, before it shrinks away again. I was recently struck by the vulnerability shown by Caitlin DeSilvey in the introductory chapter, 'Postpreservation', of her book *Curated Decay: Heritage beyond Saving* (2017). In it, as if she has lifted the words from my guilty subconscious, she writes:

> 'In my desire to be as precise as possible about the processes I observe at work, I am often forced to draw on bodies of knowledge that are outside my expertise — ecology, chemistry, materials science. I may risk failure or misinterpretation, but I seek reassurance in the awareness that potent moments always involve some form of perplexity, a recognition that forces beyond my ken are at work and that all I can do is describe what I see within the limits of my understanding.'[72]

---

72 Like DeSilvey, I too 'take heart from other thinkers who accept that there are worlds that lie beyond the borders of our ability to articulate them'. Caitlin DeSilvey, *Curated Decay: Heritage Beyond Saving* (University of Minnesota Press, 2017) p7.

It is with this sort of support, unbeknown to DeSilvey, that I'm able to write about the Dutch side of the flood at all. While I have no direct memories of the flood hitting England's east coast, there is, I think, some unnameable form of mutuality between the memories of others and my understanding of them. This though, is born out of the Thames estuary, which is keenly felt by all those who have lived with it. From the perspective of the Netherlands, however, I have had to use the support of other mediums – mediums like film that I have never really understood (and still don't fully understand) – to articulate the Dutch side of the flood story. What I have learnt in this process is that film can capture so well the distress and grandiosity of disaster. It is also a medium that can bring together the elements of personal heritage with the surrounding physical environment. I am thinking here of three films in particular: *The Beaches of Agnès* (Agnès Varda, 2009), *The Flood* (Frederic Goode, 1963) and Thomas Elsaesser's essay film *Die Sonneninsel / The Sun Island* (2017). In the latter, the happenings that befall the Elsaesser family – the downfall of the career of architect Martin Elsaesser; the creation of life on a remote island; the death of a man deeply loved by his wife; the hardship of work that she must endure through her grief and in managing, at times alone; the wild nature of the island; and not least World War II – can be seen as a reflection of the island itself. How it was cultivated, inhabited, lived and loved, abandoned in dangerous times such as through frozen winters and the war, and ultimately, permanently, deserted, so that the island should begin its process of reclaiming the land that the house was built on. The death and revival of land and of people are all elements of disaster and it is through this that I am able to get close to my subject. I have been able to visit Ouwerkerk, land once devastated by water, deprived of the animals that had grazed upon it and of the smaller ones in the soil who were so vital to its inner workings, and experience it as it is now – long cleared of the rubble from collapsed farmhouses and recovered. As can I also witness the living heritage of the people that were lost as their descendants carry on with their lives, working and living with the very same land.

After the flood, poems were published in the newspapers. Sometimes photographs came first and the poems followed, as was the case with Okke Jager's poem 'Het hergeven Woord'. In a newspaper issue from the 7th of March 1953, a photo was published of a ceiling lamp with a bible caught in its copper tentacles, an indication of how high the water reached, how it literally turned their house upside down. Hundreds of these poems are archived in Ouwerkerk at the Watersnoodmuseum[73] – folders full of poems cut out of newspapers, written by people of all ages from across the Netherlands and Belgium, and from the year of the flood continuing into present day. My favourite, by Dieuwke Parlevliet, Antwerp, February 2008, describes Zeeland, 1952, before the flood:

---

73 The Flood Museum spans across four great concrete caissons which would have looked like giant megaliths in the middle of nowhere in the year they were placed. These caissons closed the final break in the dyke, a gaping wide entrance that had been torn open with each tide, two times a day, for 10 months after the night of the flood. The gap in the dyke was 135m wide. These caissons were built by the British in WW2 and used to build Mulberry Harbours. One of these broken harbours is still out in the sands at Thorpe Bay, Southend. A local volunteer the museum told me that before the caissons were turned into a museum, they used to climb the low caissons and look over the high edge of the one sloping upwards. They would stare across the flat top of the next caisson that looked so close and yet too far to jump across. I imagine that when kids were climbing the caissons in Ouwerkerk, kids in Southend were also walking out to Mulberry Harbour in the Thorpe Bay sandbank during low tide and jumping off into the shallow water.

Zeeland 1952

By Dieuwke Parlevliet

van toen ze later nog niet wisten
en visten op mossels verkwisten
de zee was zo mooi niet de golven
de voren de vogels voedsel voor
de enkele mens zonder knoflook nog
maar niemand vervetter niemand letter
aan die lijn werd de vis gevangen
de was gehangen het leven was hard
men vloekte nochtans niet dat mag
een wonder heten van de zee het land
van toen het water later nog kwam

Recovery

*We sat in the attic in silence, we did not know what was happening
and could hear the furniture bump against the ceiling below us.*
UNKNOWN

Only a few hours after the disastrous night hard-turned into
a more disastrous morning, rescue operations were already
underway with motor-boats, helicopters, aeroplanes, Dutch
military forces and, soon after, foreign military support. Some
of the stranded managed to survive for hours, clinging to the
roofs of their houses or having climbed into a tree, waiting to be
rescued. Waiting to leave the place where they had been born,
to leave their home, possessions, their lost friends and family.[74]

Rehabilitation followed an order that seems to appear to me as
if a film playing backwards:

1. Recover the living
2. Recover the victims
3. Recover thousands of drowned farm animals
4. Depollute
5. Restore damaged dykes and dams[75]
6. Rehabilitation of roads, of communication
7. Cleaning of buildings and (temporary) building
8. Digging and draining

---

74 'Programme for the Guests of the Minister of Reconstruction and
Housing Visiting the Netherlands' 26th April–29th April (1954) p4.
Guests from Austria, Denmark, Finland, Norway and Sweden were
invited to the Netherlands to visit the gifted houses.

More than 65 countries donated money or gifted building materials to the Netherlands. The Scandinavian countries of Denmark (40), Finland (13), Norway (225) and Sweden (237) gifted entire prefabricated houses. These wooden houses, previously 'unknown, unloved'[76] by the Dutch made deep impressions. In the immediate aftermath of the flood, the Salvation Army was responsible for coordinating rescue work and collecting clothing and bedding for the displaced. Over in England along the east coast, the English Salvation Army was also working through the night to support victims. Using amphibious vehicles from boats to makeshift rafts made from planks and barrels, corps tirelessly travelled out in the dark and cold to save those who had been isolated as they sat waiting in their attics or on the roofs of their houses. On Canvey Island, there are a few heroes from the night of the flood. One is Kars Pruim, also known as 'The Mad Dutchman'. The Dutchman saved 35 lives with his barge *Tideways* over a 26-hour period. His nickname was given to him as he showed no fear when, at 2am, he saw water rush over the sea wall and immediately began to wake people up. In an interview given hours before his death in 1983, speaking with complete clarity about his memories, he said: 'You can't describe the island under water,

75 This was a monumental task. Some breaches were more than 600-feet long and water flowed through these tidal gaps twice a day. With each tide the gaps eroded further and so the mass of water became greater. On the island of Schouwen and Duiveland at Schelphoek, the breach was 525-metres wide and 40-metres deep. Twice a day 120 million cubic metres of water flowed in and out again. They couldn't close this gap and had to build a new dyke around the tidal gap using 300 concrete caissons and losing 300 hectares of fertile land to the sea. The last breach in Ouwerkerk was closed on 6th November 1953.
76 'Programme for the Guests of the Minister of Reconstruction and Housing Visiting the Netherlands' 26th April-29th April (1954) p6.

it looked like an ocean. There were no lights in any of the houses, everything was flooded out and it was freezing cold.'

Once the living had been saved, including Linda Foster, a baby he found floating in her pram who was orphaned from the floods, he spent days filling up sandbags and recovering victims.

The material goods and processes that found their way to these previously largely undisturbed areas of the Netherlands, areas of expansive farmland, can make it difficult to understand how much was lost. The sheer number of entire houses, the furniture, the bedding, the farm animals, domestic animals with their loud beating hearts,[77]

---

77 I met a man called Chris Jennings who was eight years old during the flood and living on Canvey Island. Chris's family were the landlords of The Admiral Jellicoe pub (the famous haunt of Dr Feelgood a few years later) and they lived above the pub. Chris was born there. He remembers being woken up by his parents who said to him, 'Don't worry but there's been a flood.' He tells me solemnly how many had awoken to the flood waters in their homes, people thought that they'd wet the bed or would open their front doors to be greeted by a wall of water. Chris and his family were one of the very few not to be evacuated from the island. He told a fantastic story of his role in caring for the rescued animals there. Both farm and domestic animals came to the pub, which was situated in one of the few high places of the island, and kept in a large room where Chris was asked to look after them in what seems like Noah's Ark in a pub. One account tells that 450 animals and birds were rescued: dogs, cats, horses, rabbits, fowls, pigs up in trees, canaries, parrots and a tortoise. Clearly a man with sensitivity towards animals, he tells me how their cat called Mo had had kittens. Mo and her kittens would always stay in the same place in the house, but the night before the flood, Mo took the kittens to the top floor of the building and they settled on the top shelf of the linen cupboard.

crates of oranges from South Africa, rugs from Canada, every stitch of clothing that was donated at home and abroad.

There is no space for the space created by the flood water and by the loss of livelihood and life. There are young women arriving from the north and they bring life to destroyed land. Such is the impact of a clean-up after a disaster. Life must be given to create space needed by residents to grieve.

Photo: Clasine Haringsma

Photo: Clasine Haringsma

Photo: Clasine Haringsma

Photo: Clasine Haringsma

These photographs were given to me by my friend Clasine Haringsma. Clasine's grandmother, Anne Schukking, pictured in the centre of the photo above with her hands in her pockets, was one of the young volunteers from Friesland, in her early twenties, who travelled south to the province of Zeeland. Shortly after the flood, villages were assigned an 'adoption' municipality where those affected would receive financial support but also the kind of invaluable help that Clasine's grandmother gave.

Fresh water was used to tackle the salt water. Once the last of the water was pumped out, these young women armed with buckets, brushes and mops, rolled up their sleeves to help clean-up the driftwood and hazardous mud-slathered rubble from collapsed houses.

Anne Schukking passed away in 2020.

DOGGERLAND

What this is really about is the sea at the end of your street. It is about the sea wall as a mud bank. It is everything just going. Driving across Zuiderzeeland you indicate left and keep driving across the still, dark water. There is land that was once sea and there is sea that was once land and there are the places that are in waiting. These pages are a definitive account of nothing. In writing about disaster or history, history as disaster, we can reach no final understanding of what has or not happened, nor make any predictions. If it was my intention to unthink coastlines, counties and countries in relation to a historical event, it is this that has made this book, an object, impossible to write. I am aware that with each word and each supporting quotation that I'm adding to the noise of doing and not *undoing*.

But like anything, erasure is a process. You can have a spring tide, one that pulls back and swoops forward but then, where does the water go? It swirls, seeps and erases. There is value in silt building and destroying, in ships sailing and decaying, in stories silently manifesting into a landscape. What can be found in what a flood destroys?

I want to imagine Doggerland, the sunken land that once connected Britain and mainland Europe, a bridge between England's east coast and the Netherlands that existed less than 10,000 years ago. It is the place where the storm stirred the flood. Where animals roamed beyond homesteads and past placed markers indicating how far the sea level had risen. Mammoth bones, flint and Mesolithic molars. Now, Dutch fisheries and their trawlers bring to the surface fossils of creatures that died millions of years ago. We are still re-earthing relics from underwater forests, from a land that emerged at the end of the last Ice Age and flourished into one of the most densely populated areas of Europe.

Aside from sea-level rise, it was flooding that eventually led to Doggerland's final submergence, just 8,000 years ago, as a result of the Storegga Slide. Old Norse for 'great edge', this submarine landslide caused by unstable sediment is thought to have shifted an area the size of Scotland to collapse in a single event. The seabed scar produced by the slide is considered the largest area of slope failure in the world. An ensuing tsunami devastated areas of coastline along Norway and other northern coastal regions like the Shetland Islands and eastern Scotland. Across the undulating hills of Doggerland, the water swept over the land. What we have learnt is that anything lost can be found here.

ACKNOWLEDGEMENTS

The ideas for this book started to appear a month or two after I left Southend in 2017. Not long after, I met Tom van Huisstede, who I would like to say thank you to first. Both a helpful guide, who led and supported travel to places in the Netherlands integral to the book and my acclimatisation, and my encourager, drawing me out of doubt and pushing me to write – not a job that I envied.

Thank you to the talented, patient and diligent people behind Dunlin Press, Martin Bewick and Ella Johnston, who have made this a truly positive experience. As a small, independent press, every book they publish has to count and I am grateful to them that they believed in this project.

Thank you to my brilliant parents for staying close to me and keeping us close to the Estuary.

To Carol, my favourite writer, my best critic and supporter, my genius Nan.

My thanks to John Cobbold for his early enthusiasm and for connecting me with Doreen and Tony Baker: thank you to them for sharing their memories of the flood as teenagers. Thank you to Chris Fenwick and Chris Jennings for sharing their stories.

To Metal Southend, firstly for organising their writing desks as a part of Essex Book Festival – these spaces allowed me to make a real start on the book – and later for having me on their artist residency programme in January 2020. Thank you also to James Ravinet for sharing his knowledge through trips to Foulness

Island and Canvey Island and through his work as assistant curator at Focal Point Gallery in Southend.

Through the work of the trustees and volunteers at the Foulness and Canvey Island Heritage Centres, I learnt a lot about the geographical and historical make-up of these Essex islands, particularly about the local impact of the 1953 flood – thank you. Thank you also to the Watersnoodmuseum, the National Knowledge and Remembrance Centre for the Floods of 1953, in Ouwerkerk, the Netherlands, who provided access to their excellent library and archives.

Thank you to Clasine Haringsma for sharing family photos taken by her grandmother Anne Schukking when she travelled from Friesland to Zeeland to join the clean-up effort in the days after the flood.

I would also like to extend my gratitude to Silvia Vega-Llona for allowing me to include a previously unpublished quote written by her late husband, the influential film scholar Thomas Elsaesser, in the Initial Obersvations section of this book. The quotation is from an essay by Elsaesser in 2013 that he delivered as a lecture entitled 'Contingency and Coincidence as the Ruins of Time'. I am deeply grateful to Thomas for sharing his work with me and for his advice.

The poem 'Two Tree Island' was first published in my pamphlet *Say cucumber* (Broken Sleep Books, 2019). 'Trumpet scales' is a previously commissioned poem for the book Hopelessly failing to describe my attachment, designed and published by Lucie de Bréchard (Sandberg Instituut, 2019). The section 'On rewilding' is adapted from a piece I wrote for Jo Kali and the Discourse

Programme at Rewire Festival.

To my dearest babes, Elin Keyser, Billie Manning and Rachel Angeli, for being there when I felt stuck here.

Lastly, to all those affected by the flood and their families, thank you for sharing your stories so that we do not forget them.